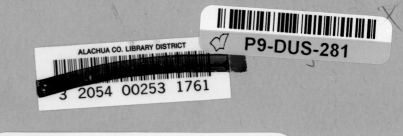

The Pacific Crest Trail

The Pacific Crest Trail
Escape to the Wilderness

ANN and MYRON SUTTON
Photographs by the Authors

J. B. LIPPINCOTT COMPANY
Philadelphia and New York

Photographs on pages 78 and 191 courtesy of
the National Park Service.

Photograph on page 85 courtesy of
the U.S. Forest Service.

Library of Congress Cataloging in Publication Data

Sutton, Ann, birth date
 The Pacific Crest Trail: escape to the wilderness.
 Bibliography: p.
 Includes index.
 1. Pacific Crest Trail. 2. Pacific States—Descrip-
tion and travel—1951-   —Guide-books. 3. Hiking—
Pacific States. 4. Trails—Pacific States. I. Sutton,
Myron, joint author. II. Title.
F851.S97   917.9′04′3   75–15920
ISBN–0–397–01061–3

To Elizabeth and Douglas Rigby

Contents

Illustrations

MAPS

Introduction

THIS BOOK IS an introduction to the Pacific Crest Trail. Or, more accurately, it introduces the reader to scenery, vegetation, wildlife, historic sites, and connecting routes of the Pacific Crest Trail system.

For although this trail is technically a single route of 2,400 miles between Mexico and Canada, it is also an avenue to side trails, secret places, startling phenomena, and adventure of many kinds. Hiking it can be pure misery or pure joy or somewhere in between.

This is not a guide that describes each pass and valley, each junction and source of water, each highway crossing. Available guidebooks do all that. We have tried here, as we did in *The Appalachian Trail*, to express some of the beauties and joys of the trail, and to tell what pitfalls might exist for unwary walkers. In these pages one may also deduce how fragile is the natural world that remains, and how significant is an appreciation and defense of it. The world has an oversupply of developed areas, but along this trail it is refreshing to find some thoroughly undeveloped—and even inhospitable—places.

Walking for pleasure has been for some time the leading form of outdoor recreation, but trails and established wilderness have not yet caught up—as witness the heavy use and consequent new regulations for control of human entry into wild areas. In the words of one forest ranger, you can find more solitude in your own backyard in Fresno than on the Pacific Crest Trail in August.

Because of this crowding, we consider other pathways that adjoin or connect with the Pacific Crest Trail. Of course, side paths may be crowded, too, and certain trail heads look like a supermarket parking lot on a Saturday afternoon. But that is all the more reason to step up the building of a nationwide network of trails as diligently as we have constructed a network of highways, to get human beings

more than ever on their feet, and to improve their health and out-
look, as hiking has been demonstrated to do.

Once on the trail, we revel that hiking requires little or no pe-
troleum energy, makes no demands for strip mining, and of all public
recreation activities has the least impact (if well planned) on the
environment. Properly constructed trails scar the landscape far less
than roads or tramways.

Of course, if we must drive long distances to reach a trail, we
use up energy, so why aren't there more trails near home? To persons interested in local trail development, there are good guiding
principles along the Pacific Crest Trail. In fact, the National Trails
System Act that established this route as a national scenic trail in
1968 also provided for systems of national recreation trails.

However, such things exist only as long as public opinion allows.
At the first suggestion of a national crisis, and especially on the
threat that automobiles may be immobilized, public opinion can
sway very rapidly away from wild places toward support of pipe-
lines, dams, and transmission lines. In the name of some national
emergency—war, defense, energy—legislators can react swiftly, opposing new trails and new wild preserves. Some do this whether or
not there is an emergency.

For that reason, it seems to us that more people should understand the real values of their public lands, so as not to cast them
away precipitately. A trail, for example, is far more than a trail. It
is a way through some of the greatest miracles on the face of the
earth. These are not always easy to see, but they must be recognized
and understood, for understanding leads to appreciation, and appreciation to protection.

The agencies administering the Pacific Crest Trail can use advice
and help, for the management problems increase as time passes.
Mining claims filed before the Wilderness Act of 1964 took effect
offer a threat. One mining company proposed to build access roads
and open up a pumice mine in the Three Sisters Wilderness, but
the Sierra Club and other conservation groups rose in unison to take
the matter to court.

There are vandalism, illegal entry of motorized vehicles, and
storm damage, but the most critical problem at this writing is heavy
use, partly by people who come to hike and partly by those who
come to live, which has so damaged portions of the trail that they
have been abandoned and travelers rerouted. The mountains attract
people who put up not only second homes but second trailers. This
brings supporting industries, and the hiker passes garages, gas
stations, and supermarkets in remote locations. What better place
than these high elevations, full of clean air and wild vistas, for housing developments? "Mountain View Acres." "Wilderness Estates."
"Alpine Village." "Leaping Deer Acres."

There are also organized group camps and club lodges, some quite elaborate. The trail environment includes railroads, radar stations, reservoirs, rifle ranges, aqueducts, power stations, work camps, ski resorts, six-cable power lines, and forest lookout towers. Given the human proclivity to multiply and to alter wild land for domestic uses, it may seem quixotic to think that a trail could be built for such a distance, much less remain wild for very long.

The trail is not always idyllic. Magnificent scenery is sometimes compromised by forest clear-cuts or by ridgetop "fuel breaks" cut through chaparral to prevent the spread of wildfires. Great avenues of forest have been cleared to accommodate transmission lines. Scars in arid country result where motorcycles and dune buggies claw up the hills and spin across the desert.

Many rivers and lakes along the way are polluted. The air on certain ridgetops near large cities can be so filled with photochemical smog that vegetation is killed. From the trail's loftier ramparts we sometimes feel as though we are looking out across a sea of adversity as smog washes up against these summits, perhaps some day to engulf them.

Some outstanding pristine areas have been severely modified by human settlement, as in the Lake Tahoe basin. In the high country are what one author calls "cow-infested meadows," on which point John Muir also had a sharp comment: "As sheep advance, flowers, vegetation, grass, soil, plenty, and poetry vanish." Inevitably the trail suffers from some of society's ubiquitous ills: overuse, congestion, litter, junk, contamination, and vandalism. The pathway is sometimes damaged by "dirt bikes" (all motor vehicles are illegal on the trail), people using shortcuts that destroy switchbacks, and gunfire that punctures or tears off markers and signs. Theft may be a problem, either by bears at campsites along the trail, or by human beings at automobiles parked near trail heads.

Land managers may have problems with livestock, as in the case of horseback parties, which require special permission and regulation. There have been calls for the elimination of domestic animals altogether from parks, wilderness areas, and national scenic trails. Unquestionably these animals pollute, trample, and erode—a special problem when they are introduced in large numbers. Of course, people also pollute, trample, and erode, so the congestion and contamination are compounded. Alpine regions and unstable meadow soils are simply too fragile to take much punishment.

But there are immensely satisfying joys and wonders, which is what this book is about. However, we couldn't hope in a single volume to describe fully the major marvels along the Pacific Crest Trail, much less the subtle ones—the call of a coyote on the desert, the hiss of hot springs in lava country, the musical glissandos of tumbling streams in the North Cascades. But many readers will know of these. We try to summarize those things hikers encounter most often: wild flora, fauna, geologic phenomena, changes of weather; and to touch upon those they encounter less frequently: moonbows, winter rime, historic sites.

In our opinion, the greatest pleasures along this trail are enjoyed not necessarily by hikers who cover forty miles a day, but by those who do seven, and especially by those who are part naturalist, poet, musician, artist. Getting the most out of this trail involves all the senses, and if we hone these senses during a hike along the Pacific Crest Trail, we are apt to return home refreshed and more able to enjoy the miraculous in the commonplace that surrounds us daily. This adds new dimensions to ordinary life and makes the days go far more rapidly than we wish.

On the other hand, some people may not get much out of hiking the Pacific Crest Trail, or else for physical reasons cannot hike it, and this book is for them as well. We regard it as a service to let readers know what the Pacific Crest Trail is not, and that hiking it could be rugged and hazardous. Disappointment awaits persons who go out expecting something the trail was not meant to provide. We include both "positive" and "negative" aspects so that prospective hikers can make up their minds. This book should thus help one ascertain whether to embark upon the trail and, if so, how to go about it—beginning with the acquisition of an inexpensive detailed guidebook.

Our hope is to make new friends for all kinds of trails—scenic, hiking, bicycling, and others—and for the hardworking people who labor publicly and privately to assure that there will always be wild glades to walk through.

We have not by any means covered every inch of the Pacific Crest Trail personally; in fact, we have deliberately left many sections undiscovered in order to leave something to anticipate on future visits. But we have visited the trail in all its regions and at different seasons, lived near it, explored side trails out from it, and interviewed persons responsible for its administration. The manuscript has been examined by Warren L. Rogers, a member of the Pacific Crest Trail Advisory Council and President of the Pacific Crest Club, which is the service club of the trail. He caught a number of errors and realigned our thinking on certain trail topics. We incorporated his and other corrections and suggestions, but the final responsibility for opinions, data, and accuracy is ours.

The authors and publishers are grateful for additional photographs, as credited.

We gratefully acknowledge the assistance of the California Department of Parks and Recreation, Forest Service of the U.S. Department of Agriculture, Bureau of Outdoor Recreation, National Park

Service, U.S. Fish and Wildlife Service, and Hale Observatories. Among many individuals who helped, the authors are especially grateful to Richard Burke, Ed Garvey, Mr. and Mrs. James Metcalf, William E. Rennebon, Marguerite Schultz, Robert Sharp, Lola F. Smith, Mr. and Mrs. John Stratton, Mr. and Mrs. Ron Strickland, Larry Sutton, and Michael Sutton.

And the three hikers of Suiattle, whose names we never knew.

ANN AND MYRON SUTTON

Hikers on Pacific Crest Trail in the Three Sisters Wilderness, Oregon

1

High Frontier

*The knapsack of custom falls off his
back with the first step he takes into these
precincts.*

Ralph Waldo Emerson, *Nature*, 1836

THEY HAD STRUGGLED for days through ice and snow. Equipped with
ice axes, coils of nylon rope over their shoulders, and 50-pound
packs, they had slipped and slid for miles, trying to get up over the
snowbound shoulder of Glacier Peak. But the snow was too deep.
Trail markings lay buried. The July sun had melted the surface
enough to make it slick and dangerous.

The mountains of western Washington lay under one of the
heaviest blankets of snow and ice in memory. With a wet, cloudy
spring and cool summer, the highest points along the Pacific Crest
Trail would remain buried and closed through most or all of the
hiking season.

So the three hikers, tired and dirty, made a painful decision: to
abandon their trek, at least temporarily, and get down out of the
mountains. They descended Milk Creek, a roaring white-water
mountain stream, and dropped rapidly from the regions of ice and
snow to luxuriant forests of fir and cedar. Surrounded by carpets
of sphagnum moss and meadows burgeoning with lilies and columbines, they felt a sense of relief.

From slippery snow to slippery mud: their heavy boots now
splashed in melting water that trickled and tumbled down the trail.
At times the path was blocked by fallen trees or made hazardous
with rocks and roots, and the hikers had to maneuver carefully in
order not to be thrown off balance by their heavy packs.

Mile after mile they descended, switchbacking to the Suiattle

River, crossing the stream on a bridge, and walking a final mile to the parking lot. There each hiker placed her pack beside a rock and propped herself up against it for a rest.

And that is how we found them as we came down the Suiattle River trail ourselves, after a day of hiking and picture making.

"Could you take us to the nearest ranger station?" they asked.

With their gear and ours aboard, the car seemed to sag under the weight of so many packs, ropes, axes, supplies, and bodies. Then it took nearly 30 miles of gravel, dirt, and asphalt road to reach the ranger station, from which the girls sent forth their calls to friends to come and pick them up.

At no time did they speak with anything but enthusiasm for the trail and mountains. Notwithstanding the ice and snow, each would be ready to tackle another section of the trail tomorrow, resupplied and reequipped. Nothing dampened their spirits. Their only disappointment was having to leave.

And there you have a more or less typical hiker on the Pacific Crest Trail, one able to take considerable punishment and descend dead tired—yet alive and tuned to the joys of wild country.

Could it happen to anyone? Maybe. A trail experience such as the one these three girls endured is not for everyone. They happened to select some of the most difficult parts of the trail after a season of especially heavy snowfall. Most of the other 2,400 miles of trail between Mexico and Canada are, in summer at least, more negotiable. And though the Pacific Crest Trail itself passes through some of the most attractive scenery and beautiful forests in North America, the side trails open up a multitude of additional landscapes.

Originally the trail was intended to be a path through wild country to scenic places and natural landscapes. That must have seemed impossible, even back in 1932 when the idea was born, because even then roads were being built into the mountains and private dwellings erected.

In the earliest part of the twentieth century, the concept of long trails was more or less a novelty, although there had been "wilderness roads" in history, and the Indians had developed trails that became "traces." The Europeans had long made an art of walking and established youth hostel routes as well as outing clubs.

In the United States a few extended trails had come into existence, such as the Crawford Path in New Hampshire. Vermont's Long Trail, in the Green Mountains, was started about 1910, and the dream of the Appalachian Trail had already begun. As early as 1920 the U.S. Forest Service began surveying trails in the Cascade Range of Washington and Oregon and the Sierra Nevada of California.

Clinton C. Clarke, of Pasadena, California, made what was apparently the first proposal for a connected trail along the crest of these ranges, suggesting in 1932 to both the Forest Service and the National Park Service that a wilderness trail be built between Mexico and Canada. The idea fell into a fertile environment, partly because of the momentum of the Appalachian Trail, which at that time was nearing its initial completion. Most of the Pacific Crest Trail route, as first delineated, went through national parks and forests. (Eighty percent of it still crosses publicly owned land.) Work on certain portions was authorized by park and forest administrators. Workers from Civilian Conservation Corps camps constructed sections of the John Muir Trail, which was later included in the Pacific Crest Trail System. The Oregon Skyline Trail was also being laid out.

Warren L. Rogers, of Santa Ana, California, a member of the Pacific Crest Trail Council, relates: "When Clarke and I worked on the list of landmarks, the route selected avoided development areas and was planned to cross roads as directly as possible. The original concept was to reach scenic areas, not the most direct route through the mountains."

In 1935, Clarke published a booklet entitled "The Pacific Crest Trail, Canada to Mexico," in which he called for help to protect the trail from commercial exploitation. "There has been a serious overdevelopment of road building and recreation camp projects in our mountain wildernesses," he wrote. "Our primitive nature wonderlands are fast disappearing before the encroachments of our civilization."

Hoping to arouse wide interest in wild country, he described the scenery, flora, and fauna, and appealed to youth organizations such as Girl Scouts, Boy Scouts, YMCA, and mountain and outing clubs to place on their summer programs trips of exploration along the trail. He thought that the route should be a focus for the development of outdoor leagues such as had been successful in Russia up to that time.

In our hurry-scurry world of machines, noise and distractions [he wrote], the mind becomes confused and our sense of values is lost. Throw down your sleeping-bag beneath a pine high on a mountain side, and get acquainted with that vast world of God's creatures that are more and more being banished from our consciousness. Peace and contentment come, events that yesterday seemed so vital shrink to their true worth, and we return to the slavery of our inhuman world with enlightened mind and revivified soul.

The loss of primitive areas around Los Angeles particularly impelled the movement. Clarke deplored the fact that the mountains had begun to look like city subdivisions, and said that in all that fine

Temporary trail route along Oregon country road

back country it was hardly possible to get away from the "honk of the auto horn or the smell of the hot dog."

Before long, a Pacific Crest Trail System Conference was established to manage and publicize the trail. It set three principal tasks: to preserve wilderness, to encourage public use, and to promote appreciation of the outdoors.

By 1935 the route had been laid out in seven more or less connecting trails: Desert Crest, Sierra, John Muir, Tahoe-Yosemite, Lava Crest, Oregon Skyline, and Cascade Crest. By 1941, Clarke claimed, "the trail was a complete wilderness trail, except for a few detours, mapped and signed." And this only four years after completion of the Appalachian Trail.

But a great deal of work had to be done on both trails, for "completion" was really accomplished in dream only, and certain sections still had to be constructed. Much of the Pacific Crest Trail still does not follow its officially established route, which will probably not be completed until 1980. Until then, alternate and temporary routes are being used.

If the Spanish poet Antonio Machado assumed correctly that paths are made by walking, then the Pacific Crest Trail got a good start when forty teams of youngsters hiked the entire distance in volunteer relays during the summers of 1935 through 1938. Sponsored by some thirty YMCAs along the West Coast, these hikers carried from Mexico to Canada a logbook in which were recorded comments by people encountered. Thus was completed the first exploration of the route of the Pacific Crest Trail, and the first major public information about it.

Later, war clouds shadowed progress, but the Forest Service and National Park Service made as much progress as possible on trail sections under their jurisdiction. In the 1960s a report entitled "Trails for America" was issued by the U.S. Government, and after that came the National Trails System Act of 1968. This act cleared the way officially for the establishment of long-distance national scenic trails. According to the act, these would provide maximum outdoor recreation potential and would conserve nationally significant scenic, historic, or cultural qualities of areas through which they passed. The act also authorized the establishment of connecting or side routes so as to provide additional points of access to the major scenic trails.

The Appalachian Trail and the Pacific Crest Trail were designated as the first two national scenic trails, and the act authorized studies of other trails for similar designations, including the Oregon Trail, Natchez Trace, Santa Fe Trail, El Camino Real in Florida, Mormon Trail, Alaska gold-rush trails, and cattle trails of the old Southwest, including the Chisholm Trail.

The Secretary of the Interior was given responsibility for administering the Appalachian Trail. The Secretary of Agriculture assumed administration of the Pacific Crest Trail. Both federal departments devise regulations, limitations, cooperative agreements, and other management rules. To provide for citizen involvement in planning and operation, the law authorized establishment of advisory councils, each not to exceed thirty-five persons, including members appointed to represent federal agencies as well as state governments, private organizations, landowners, and others administering the lands through which the trail passes.

The Advisory Council for the Pacific Crest Trail represents youth and camping organizations, conservation groups, mountaineer clubs, commercial associations, and property owners. It meets once a year and considers such matters as trail location, standards, markers, rights-of-way, construction priorities, and the management and use of the trail. The location and identification of the trail route was published in the *Federal Register* for January 30, 1973.

A Pacific Crest Club, sponsored by Camp Research Foundation, Box 1907, Santa Ana, California 92702, was organized to provide a means through which individuals and families could relate to the trail. The club's objectives are principally education for proper recreational use, conservation of the trail, and volunteer work on trail construction under Forest Service supervision.

Layout and construction of the route may seem random or haphazard, but a great deal of thought and planning go into the process. Odd as it may seem, keeping the trail environment natural is a complicated task, and the path must be designed initially to avoid as much manipulated landscape as possible.

In California two thirds of the trail has been constructed; elsewhere hikers must follow temporary alternate routes along country roads or other trails. In Oregon and Washington the trail is about 95 percent complete.

Actual construction of the trail is an immense task. The route covers nearly 17 degrees of latitude and varies in elevation from tidewater to 13,200 feet, which offers a tremendous variation in climatic patterns and a challenge to both construction and maintenance.

Rights-of-way being obtained across private lands can be anywhere from fifty yards to a mile wide, depending upon the terrain and in keeping with criteria established by the National Trails System Act. Grades are usually kept to 10 percent or less. Maintaining these standards is sometimes costly, and trail construction can exceed $10,000 a mile. That kind of budgetary allocation for outdoor recreation is hard for administering agencies to justify if Congress happens to be in a cost-cutting mood during inflationary periods.

Though generally a crest-line route, the trail does not follow

Forest floor of sphagnum moss and twinflower, Glacier Peak Wilderness, Washington

high ridges throughout. Far from it. The hiker goes through miles of forests, lowlands, wetlands, meadows, or desert. Whatever the condition of the pathway, broad sweeps in elevation mean wide temperature variations that could be troublesome to hikers, even in summer. At high elevations, summer is fleeting anyway, and the nights are seldom frost-free. So a cold, windy trip can ensue. In places the hiker traverses snowfields and passes near scores of glaciers or perpetually frozen lakes.

At the other extreme, part of the trail goes through the Mojave Desert, where the searing summer heat may rise above 120 degrees. Even in a single day, temperatures may be near 100 degrees in the daytime and close to freezing at night. Thus a hiker can sometimes be hot and dusty and miserable. Or cold and wet and miserable.

Unlike the Appalachian Trail, the Pacific Crest Trail has few huts, shelters, lean-tos, or cabins, principally because much of it crosses established wilderness areas where such structures are prohibited by law. A hiker must be self-reliant. However, considering the availability of sturdy, lightweight tents these days, traditional shelters are not perhaps as necessary as they used to be. Indeed, Appalachian Trail shelters have attracted destructive concentrations of hikers, and the use of some of these structures has been banned for that reason.

Along certain sections of the Pacific Crest Trail, the vegetation is scanty, especially at elevations above tree line. In the desert, a hiker has Joshua trees for company. But elsewhere the forest is so dense that a person will feel as though he is walking down a cathedrallike aisle struck only by a few faint rays of sunlight. Much of the way is through chaparral, that densely packed, highly flammable shrub community that literally confines the hiker to established routes whether he likes it or not.

By far the most striking vegetative aspect of the Pacific Crest Trail is the abundance of wildflowers. In proper season the desert becomes a living mass of poppies and other species, while the Cascade Range almost glows with concentrations of alpine species.

Despite human encroachment, there is much vegetation and wildlife. Deer, bear, and possibly mountain goats may be sighted occasionally; squirrels and chipmunks abound. Birds are commonplace in some lowland forests, rare in others; they also occur near the highest summits and in the lowest deserts. Even though elevations vary widely, the Pacific Crest Trail passes through regions abundant with reptiles and amphibians. Toads and frogs are the most often seen, and snakes occur all the way from Mexico to Canada. In warmer and drier places, the hiker must beware of rattlesnakes, though the chance of encountering poisonous reptiles is remote.

Hikers expecting to find the trail a boulevard may be disappointed. In some places there is no trail at all, not even a temporary one—although directions in guidebooks show how to breach these gaps. The trail may be difficult to follow because animal trails or logging roads converge with it, and hikers can make a wrong turn with the greatest of ease.

Occasionally the trail is rather hair-raising, what with knife-edge ridges and steep slopes. The path is frequently wet, muddy, dusty, or deeply rutted. Where maintenance lags and the trail becomes overgrown, an unwary hiker unable to see the ground might step on a rattlesnake.

In many places, it is only when the snow melts that maintenance can begin, so park and forest crews may not be able to cover all parts of the trail even by the end of summer. They cannot get into some portions of the trail until August, if at all.

Then there may be so many washouts to fill or fallen trees to clear away (some huge enough to require major efforts at removal) that the job cannot be accomplished before the crews must be terminated or the weather turns bad again.

Maintenance is only one factor in trail upkeep. Protection of trail and environment must be taken into account and regulations enforced. Permits are required along most of the trail for overnight travel in parks, forests, and wilderness areas. In some places, fires are prohibited because of extremely dry conditions during summer. No hunting, trapping, or collecting of natural objects may be done in state and national parks.

Of course, conditions are not destined to remain the same in an environment so exposed to the elements. If there were to be a slight reduction in worldwide temperatures, it is conceivable that glaciers could advance and cover portions of the trail as it is now routed.

Any of the hundreds of volcanic vents, fissures, cones, and craters beside the trail could erupt and bury the trail under immense weights of lava. Rock slides, avalanches, and tree blowdowns could take their toll. But perhaps the most likely change will come as a result of human activity, unless worldwide population and environmental contamination are brought under control.

As for more immediate hazards along temporary routes, the walker may have to traverse narrow logging roads that have no shoulders, a tricky situation when logging trucks roar around a corner. Quite often the route contours gently around topographic features, allowing progress without much climbing or descending. But other parts of the trail require almost excruciating up-and-down hiking at elevations between 8,000 and 13,000 feet. Obviously, hikers should be in good physical shape to take that—and may want to hike on less strenuous trails in order to "work up" to this one.

The Pacific Crest Trail system is full of extremes, often unpredictable. Much of it is dry. In the desert portions, planning is essential before a hiker tries to negotiate about 30 miles of burning terrain where no water is to be had. One solution, of course, is to walk at night, but it is quite possible to get thirsty after sundown, too; and certainly inexperienced hikers should never risk becoming lost in the dark.

Or the trail may be wet. Hikers must cross many a stream by hopping on boulders or by wading. Even when rain is not falling, the accumulation of moisture from fog on trailside shrubbery keeps a hiker's shoes and apparel dripping, an effective way to get thoroughly wet in perfectly clear weather.

The days may be hot, dry, calm. Or high winds and fiercely blowing dust may become a hazard. In cold weather, strong icy winds can howl at hurricane force on the ridges and literally force a hiker to shelter. Winds may even continue to rage at night.

Biting flies, mosquitoes, and other insects will test the hiker's stamina and patience. So will the search for good places to stop and rest.

Wild campsites are available, and developed campgrounds may frequently be found near the trail. But in a few places no camping is permitted at all, and a hiker must watch for No Trespassing signs, forest closures, construction, or fire hazards.

And noise? The trail is mostly quiet, justly famed for its solitude. Yet there are places where one gets an earful of industrialization, as in the roar of traffic along interstate highways and in the blasts of locomotive whistles on transcontinental railroads. Sometimes the solitude is shattered by sonic booms, especially along the southern part of the trail near military installations.

For all its "negative aspects," though, the trail is overwhelmingly delightful. A hiker frequently experiences the exhilaration of feeling on top of the world as he hikes high ridges above glaciated canyons, with the forested world spread out below.

For most of the distance there are magnificent views and high country panoramas. In the heavily forested northern parts, however, one travels for miles without seeing beyond the most immediate trees. Of course, much may be seen within the woods because the ecosystems are very rich, but we sometimes have tantalizing glimpses of distant mountain ranges and become very anxious to see them better.

If the forests are badly cut over in places, elsewhere they are growing back. And even without panoramic views, the trail is an entity of its own, not just a platform from which to see the landscape. One may revel in a hike that has no destination at all—or even a single panorama. There is plenty of interest along the trailside.

Some coveted campsites lie next to waterfalls. Good fishing may be found in streams, lakes, reservoirs. There are splendid places for

Mount Hood, Oregon

layover days to allow swimming, fishing, relaxing, resupplying, and repacking. If trouble arises, park and forest rangers assigned to certain stretches of the trail or to wilderness areas may be called upon for assistance.

The senses respond to abundant pleasures. Many trail sections are redolent with savory aromas of mint, pine, and sage. A symphony of sounds pours from birds, from wind sifting through the trees, and from cascading rivulets. Natural foods, such as strawberries and blueberries, flourish in places, and can be abundant, as Oregon huckleberry hunters know.

A person may exercise a right increasingly restricted these days: to wander at random. This aimless roving may be contrary to the principles of industrial progress, but for a wanderer nothing is better calculated to clear the mind and enlarge the vision.

Along much of the route the wayfarer can go where he pleases—forward or back, off the trail, into towns for supplies and out again—accountable to no one and completely without a schedule or itinerary. One day we watched a hiker emerge from a restaurant in a mountain town, hoist his pack, smile contentedly, and move down the street toward the mountain trails.

We once passed a commercial tree farm which displayed a sign that read: "A Producing Forest." One might infer from this that a wild forest is also highly productive—of natural beauty, wildlife, water, poetry, and music.

Up on the trail we feel more in command of our destiny. We human beings are at best weak and fragile; the great cities and dual highways are symptoms of that. In those metropolises below, unpredictable things go wrong, whereas amid these peaks and forests we rather know what will happen. Or we don't know—and for once we don't mind that we don't know.

Up here we have a better picture of the frantic human need to sustain today's level of life by pushing at the upper limits of the earth's resources. But nature, too, is fragile. And it becomes more clear that the modern messiahs are those opposing blind progress, and that success must eventually prevail for persons attempting to make the earth a sanctuary for all life.

On top of the crests, with their stunning views, one could scarcely have a better introduction to the geology of western North America. The trail leads through classic examples of earth-making phenomena; exhibitions of glaciation and volcanism are scarcely equaled anywhere. The world's second highest waterfall lies just a few miles off the trail. The route follows one of the earth's most celebrated, and death-dealing, fracture zones. There are also geothermal basins, basalt palisades, and various kinds of caves.

One sees classic ecological events, such as the struggle of plants to advance on alpine terrain, on pumice deserts, and on lava flows. In short, hiking the Pacific Crest Trail is such an adventure that, as John Muir would say, the mind is fertilized and stimulated and developed like sun-fed plants.

Any traveler who wants his mind to take root in fundamental details of the underlying earth or the life upon it will find self-guiding nature trails, particularly in park and forest sites. Museums exist at various distances off the main route, and the restored ghost towns and mining enterprises constitute a living lesson in American history.

Along the route now followed by this trail came Spanish explorers, trappers, traders, soldiers, priests, and scientists as much as four centuries ago. Into these mountains prospectors rushed for gold, their adventures recorded eloquently (and hilariously, as we shall see) by such as Dame Shirley.

Here the Donner and Duckwall parties tried to conquer the heavy snows of winter. Here Lewis and Clark made their historic penetration of the dangerous, mysterious, beautiful Pacific Northwest. Here began the first competitive sport skiing in the Western Hemisphere.

The trail passes through Indian country, including that of the Diegueños of southern California, Sierra Nevada tribes, Maidu, Klamath, Yakima, and others. The handiwork, tools, and paraphernalia of these early tribes remain on display in federal, state, and local museums near the trail route.

Despite the possibility of battling the elements and encountering hazards along the way, thousands of hikers each year use the Pacific Crest Trail. Probably the most common type of use is the pleasant weekend walk or overnight hike and camp-out, but some people test their endurance by attempting to hike the entire trail in a single summer. This is a splendid challenge, but it has disadvantages: a hiker cannot see each part of the trail at its best. Either there is too much water or snow, or the flowers are not out, or the grass, rather than being fresh and green, lies seared and browned by the summer sun.

Besides, the pace required to cover so much distance in a relatively short time is too fast for some people. "I just don't understand the twenty-five-mile-a-day endurance hikers who plow along and don't seem to enjoy it," one patrol ranger told us. "I would prefer to hike along at five or ten miles a day and take a greater interest in the wilderness surroundings."

Whatever the hiker's intention, there are certain details that should be contemplated in advance. Much of the route lies at high

Eagle Creek, Columbia River Gorge, Oregon

elevation, and the traveler may go for miles without dropping below 10,000 feet. Warm clothing is thus required if the hiker is to be comfortable at cool temperatures, including those on summer nights.

Hikers at upper elevations should be in good physical condition. This implies not only stamina to take the sometimes grueling climbs, but a reservoir of energy to sustain the body in case of accident.

And accidents are quite possible. The trail can be rough and rocky, which means tricky footing. In early spring there may be deep snow in the north country, so ropes and ice axes should be a part of the hiker's equipment. "Early spring" on this trail can last through the end of July.

Properly equipped, an outdoor recreationist can enjoy the Pacific Crest Trail in any season. Though most often used in summer, it passes through places that receive some of the heaviest snowfall in North America and may be buried for long periods of time. But the southern reaches are more open and hospitable in winter, though even parts of them can be clogged with snow. The lower elevations, of course, are open most or all the year.

Some people like to travel in deep snow, which is rewarding and fun, but such is not for everyone. Following the trail can be difficult and dangerous when markers cannot be seen. Also, weather changes may be sudden and treacherous.

Other possibilities are offered by side trails. In this book, we describe—or at least mention—some of the most important destinations a hiker may enjoy by taking off a day or two and leaving the main trail. Examples include the Cuyamaca Rancho State Park, Hale Observatories, Anza-Borrego Desert State Park, Yosemite Valley, and the historic mining areas of Julian, Columbia, and Plumas-Eureka —all in California—plus Crater Lake in Oregon and Lake Chelan in Washington.

In more than one instance, side trails pass through more magnificent vales than the Pacific Crest Trail itself, an example being the Eagle Creek Trail down into the Columbia River Gorge in Oregon.

However, certain side trails may be less maintained and thus hazardous, so persons with large and heavy backpacks should make inquiries before hiking those trails that are steep and narrow and difficult of passage. It is also easy to get lost on them if logging operations obliterate the routes or markers.

All the possible confusion and distress make clear that prospective hikers should (1) plan ahead and (2) obtain guidebooks. Just getting to trail heads can be a major expedition. In one instance, a person must drive 90 miles from the nearest motel, then hike 10 miles to reach the Pacific Crest Trail. Developed campgrounds are closer, of course, but one often needs maps to find them.

Maps and detailed information may be obtained from parks

and forests along the way; addresses are given in Appendix 2. Long-distance hikers must watch for sources of food and water, which are sometimes far apart. The northernmost 184 miles of the Pacific Crest Trail, for example, contain no supply points whatever, and the hiker must arrange his own system of provisioning.

Trail camping is sometimes permitted only at designated areas, so the hiker must learn where these are. Given the proliferation of human beings, certain camp spots may be closed due to overuse, or are so crowded that alternate sites must be selected.

Camping at high elevations may be exhilarating, but it loses some of its appeal when the camper discovers that there is no water up there, especially in late summer or during drought. Firewood is also scarce or nonexistent at high elevations and is better left unburned anyway. The traveler should carry a portable stove; indeed, portable cookstoves are required along certain parts of the trail.

Other questions to ponder in advance are where to go and what to do. For this, guidebooks are helpful in preliminary planning and can be taken along on a trip. One of the most complete is a series called *Pacific Crest Trail Pocket Guide* by Warren L. Rogers, composed of five volumes covering Washington, Oregon, Northern California, Central California, and Southern California. These are available from Camp Research Foundation, Box 1907, Santa Ana, California 92702.

Two splendid guides have been published by the Wilderness Press: *The Pacific Crest Trail, Volume 1: California* by Thomas Winnett, and *The Pacific Crest Trail, Volume 2: Oregon and Washington*, by Jeff Schaffer and Bev and Fred Hartline. Guidebooks to specific parts of the route, such as the Oregon Skyline Trail, and to side trails, are also available.

These guides give a wealth of information not only on the main route, but on connecting paths; for example, at some junctions a hiker can take trails that circle whole mountain systems, such as Mount Hood, Mount Rainier, and Mount Adams.

The books also tell what restrictions and regulations are in effect on state and federal areas en route. They describe campsites good and bad, give choices of routes in case a hiker prefers shorter, longer, or more scenic paths, or those more moist or gentle in passage.

They reveal what could be critical information. When a sign says "No trespassing, hunting or fishing—under penalty of law," it is difficult to know whether hikers have authority to pass. Other information given includes distances between settlements, places where supplies may be obtained, and, most important, sources and reliability of water.

Even with guidebooks, one must be alert to find a way through complex terrain. One direction, for example, reads: "Continue west, above the south bank of the East Fork of the West Fork of the Mojave River. . . ."

Park and forest maps reveal unusual points of interest, including nature reserves such as that at Crane Prairie, in central Oregon, site of the largest nesting colony of ospreys in the Northwest.

Even the best maps and guidebooks, however, cannot save the hiker who is untrained and ill prepared in the face of hazards along the trail. Getting lost is easy and can be thoroughly enjoyable—but not if a hiker is down to the last scrap of food or drop of water. The Pacific Crest Trail is by no means marked throughout—or so constructed that you can't miss it. You can, you will, and you may as well expect to lose some time now and then. Certain parts are signed poorly, inaccurately, or not at all, and with all the crisscrossing animal paths, side trails, motor routes, and logging roads a hiker is bound to go astray.

Other trail hazards could include getting shot at by hunters or by persons who shoot at anything that moves. One must beware of falling trees, solar radiation, icy patches, loose rocks, roots, avalanche chutes, flooded rivers, high winds, blizzards, lightning, forest fires, geothermal areas, and excessive cold. Hikers who stray off the trail must watch for unstable rims of canyons, hidden drop-offs, and dangerous ledges.

Wildlife is not a hazard, except that bears and rattlesnakes, if molested, can strike back. Mosquitoes may cause irritation unless the traveler is protected against them. Plants to be avoided include poison oak and such exceptionally thorny species as devil's club.

Still, with all the potential hazards, and the need to be prepared for them, one should not be overawed. "Fear not . . . to try the mountain passes," wrote John Muir in *The Mountains of California.* "They will kill care, save you from deadly apathy, set you free, and call forth every faculty into vigorous, enthusiastic action."

Not every hiker, alas, has come and gone as Muir did, leaving only footprints and eloquent words. The behavior of human beings hiking the trail has become a problem compounded by large numbers of hikers.

The traveler may encounter noisemakers, litter throwers, tree choppers, short-cutters, flower pickers, polluters, vandals, and lawbreakers. Incidents involving poorly behaved travelers have compelled landowners along side trails and approach routes to erect a forest of No Trespassing signs. Certain lakeshores have been so littered with trash that the lakes have had to be closed to public use.

Besides crowding, sanitation has been a problem at high elevations where there is little soil and no trees.

All this has made necessary a permit system and controlled

access, as has happened already at Mount Whitney. It may be painful to give up that old tradition, the western campfire, and resort to backpack stoves, but such is the consequence of excess human use of the trail route.

"Car campers" is a name given to persons who camp in places easily approached by automobiles. The resultant concentrations have not been good for the environment, and users of wilderness trails are particularly disappointed in the deterioration of the landscape. They are led to believe that persons who make the least effort to get into the wilderness are those who make the least effort to preserve it.

Hence the restrictions. Yet restrictions on human behavior and entry are not necessarily antisocial; in these places one loves not human beings less but wilderness more.

And that is why the Pacific Crest Trail, for all its problems, remains so popular. Its very existence as a priceless part of the American scene, and as a superb introduction into wild and original America, is a tribute to the enterprise, diligence, and hard work of trail believers.

Notwithstanding attacks on its environment, the trail still leads through wild and beautiful lands, and the impressions one gets along it are as enduring as the solid granite over which much of it passes.

For one thing, the Pacific Crest Trail is a lake trail, particularly in its northern half. It passes among countless high-elevation glacial lakes and ponds, and even where lavas are porous and waters normally sink out of sight, there are abundant bodies of water, including that most lovely of all—Crater Lake.

The most memorable sights to us are crystal-clear streams, alpine flowers, the desert in bloom, the Columbia River Gorge, and snow-covered volcanic peaks coming out of storm clouds or dissolving in the darkening gold of sunset.

We remember distinctive American place names: Dread and Terror Ridge, Nip and Tuck Lakes, Wits End, Tipsoo Trail, Perspiration Point, Horsethief Canyon, Humbug Ridge, Bullion Basin, Pickhandle Gap, Three Fools Peak, and the Devils Backbone.

From one end of the trail to the other, a recurring experience is that of walking through forested dells lined with ferns. Other impressions come rolling in, one on another as in a montage, sometimes confusing. We can still see woodpeckers dive-bombing scrub jays, bees clustered around mint flowers, and steam clouds rising from Boiling Springs Lake. How often does a gust of pine-scented wind bring down on us a shower of hemlock needles?

We watch the purple-tinted heads of grass waving in the breeze, a yellow dragonfly perched on a flowering stalk of beargrass. Along parts of the trail we walk on pure glass, the volcanic glass of ob-

Waldo Lake and Diamond Peak, Oregon

sidian. And on pond surfaces we see reflections of tall cliffs and rolling clouds.

We retain a blur of spotted rocks, too, for they are everywhere: white granite speckled with black crystals of mica, or boulders encrusted with dark circular patches of lichens, which in turn are spotted with tiny dots of chartreuse and yellow species of lichens.

One would need multiple lives to enjoy all these, plus thousands of other impressions along the Pacific Crest Trail. Like any precious jewel, this simple trail through complex natural scenes merits special measures for safekeeping.

The mission set by Clinton Clarke in 1932 remains now as valid and worthy of carrying out as it did then: "To maintain and defend for the benefit and enjoyment of nature lovers the Pacific Crest Trailway as a primitive wilderness pathway in an environment of solitude, free from the sights and sounds of a mechanically disturbed nature."

Come along, then, through hundreds of miles of open-air cathedrals, moon landscapes, icebound sculpture gardens, granite temples, and nearly impenetrable cloud forests. And back in time—among Indians, mountain scouts, and miners.

For it is not one trail, but many.

2

Desert Crest

Caminante, son tus huellas
el camino, y nada más;
caminante, no hay camino,
se hace camino al andar.
Al andar se hace camino,
y al volver la vista atrás
se ve la senda que nunca
se ha de volver a pisar.
Caminante, no hay camino,
sino estelas en la mar. *

Antonio Machado, *Proverbios*
y Cantares, 1964

THE PACIFIC CREST TRAIL gets off to a rousing start. From the Mexican boundary, 30 miles southeast of San Diego, at nearly 3,000 feet elevation, it twists to the north through mountainous, bouldery terrain so thickly beset with chaparral that one would scarcely expect a lizard to find a way through.

The ridges bristle with granite outcrops smoothed and rounded by erosion, in places looking as though some giant had hurled a cluster of huge ivory bowling balls across the countryside. These head-high, house-high boulders are part of a deep-seated granite mass that weathering agents such as wind and running water have uncovered and are proceeding to disintegrate.

* Traveler, your footsteps are
  the path, and nothing else;
  traveler, there is no path,
  a path is made by walking.
  Walking makes the path,
  and on looking back
  we see a trail that never
  can be walked again.
  Traveler, there is no path,
  Only a wake in the sea.

Cuyamaca Rancho State Park, California

For 170 miles the trail passes among ridges, domes, and canyons in the northern end of the Peninsular Ranges, an extension of the mountains of Baja California. The once-molten rock cooled so slowly that it crystallized into coarse-grained granite and gabbro, and in places the mountains have been mined for gold and precious minerals, including high-quality gems.

In fair weather or foul, a hike through this region is like being on center stage in some Wagnerian drama. Low clouds sometimes sail over the passes from San Diego and the Pacific Ocean, and fogs creep up the valleys as misty rains sweep in sheets across the boulder fields. At such times, the rain-washed soil and rock emit earthy odors of wetted clay, and certain shrubs produce an ultrasweet aroma that pervades every crevice and haunts every vale. Thus, right off, the trail begins to challenge the senses.

Mud and pools of water must be waded through, of course, but a hiker on the Pacific Crest Trail may as well get used to it. Anyone who hikes the entire trail has to ford streams, cross swampy meadows, or traverse melting patches of snow. Mists obscure the sun, reducing it to an incandescent glow that bathes the countryside in orange hues.

Eventually the clouds depart, and solar radiation passes nearly unfiltered through a clear sky. When that happens, hikers with sensitive skins had better take precautions. Even a hat may not be enough when the sunlight is especially intense; solar radiation reflected from bright rocks can cause problems.

Some of the route along here has been laid out temporarily on country roads, which means that the hiker passes fences, cattle, housing developments, transmission lines, stores, cars, and No Trespassing signs and may begin to wonder what is so great about this "wilderness trail."

Then comes relief as the route heads up into mountains. Looking back, the traveler can trace the winding courses of streams or underground moisture by following the curving lines of cottonwood trees below; in November these lines become bright yellow, like outpourings of molten gold.

In its southerly reaches the trail passes groves of sycamore trees, which would be universally revered as works of art were they not so common. A perceptive observer may stop to marvel at innumerable designs and patterns in the white and gray mottled trunks, at sunlight reflecting from the twisted arms, or at leaf shadows falling against the bark. For such reasons, some hikers may not get as far along the trail each day as planned. They soon learn the worthlessness and tyranny of schedules.

To make matters worse—or better, as the case may be—San Diego and Riverside Counties happen to be laden with precious minerals; from pegmatite veins have come gem-quality tourmaline, spodumene, beryl, topaz, garnet, and quartz. This is not to say that the Pacific Crest Trail is lined with such crystalline treasures or that the trail even goes through the best mineral localities. But travelers with a touch of rock-hound fever will have a problem trying to keep their eyes on trail, rocks, minerals, sycamores, jays, and clouds at once.

The sudden shriek of scrub jays may startle listeners in these oak woods, but the flashing blue, white, and brown feathers and the sweeping glide are pure art and ballet. The roadrunner can also be seen above the boulders, lifting itself from a rocky perch and falling into the wind along a swooping trajectory to the valley below.

Mile after mile the trail leads north through chaparral, an association of chamise, scrub oak, manzanita, sagebrush, ceanothus, buckthorn, yucca, deerweed, mountain mahogany, and hundreds of other kinds of plants. Chaparral—from the Mexican *chaparra*, a plant community where evergreen scrub oak predominates—covers more than 8 million acres in California, and may be found in other parts of the Southwest as well as in Mexico. It is perhaps most frequently encountered on steep terrain, if only because it has been removed from gentler landscapes to make way for human dwellings and forest management schemes. At its upper limits, chaparral enters pine forests, with islands of one in zones of the other.

Botanists consider chaparral one of the most fire-susceptible plant communities anywhere, and the evidence is sometimes starkly apparent. The Pacific Crest Trail breaks out onto open ridges of charred and twisted stalks—remains of chaparral consumed in wildfires.

Eventually the hiker climbs into higher country, where pines and mountain mahogany offer a little shade. At about 5,000 feet elevation, the trail enters groves of Jeffrey pine, whose trunks, encased in reddish-brown bark plates, resemble columns of Roman temples at sunset. They are straight and unblemished, contrasting with blue sky, dark shadows, or winter snow. The trees are sometimes attacked by flatheaded borers, but most live for a century or two. Their contributions to wildlife continue after death, for we see them riddled with woodpecker holes, and if the dead trees are not cleared away by human beings or consumed in fire they will decay and enrich the mountain soil.

The trail rises into the Laguna Mountains, a tilted fault block whose eastern escarpment overlooks the desert. Through Cleveland National Forest, past black oak groves, squawbush, coffeeberry, serviceberry, chokecherry, and incense cedar, the hiker tops out at 6,000 feet and begins to get an eagle's view of southern California.

Anyone who stays very long must also adapt to an eagle's environment. The air is cool or cold, and winds roaring up over the ridge may approach 100 miles an hour. Lightning blasts the trees. In fall and winter, snow smothers the land and ice grips the

Granite country along Mexico-California boundary

Badlands in Anza-Borrego Desert State Park

soil and vegetation. In the face of such natural phenomena, manzanita and mountain mahogany on the outermost cliffs cannot achieve their usual stature, and are here low-growing and well pruned. This permits the traveler an unobstructed view of ridges dropping dizzily below, their edges barely touched with lines of light as the sun descends.

Light blazes beyond, however: the badlands of the Anza-Borrego Desert, where nearly half a million acres have been preserved as California's largest state park.

This offers a good opportunity for a side trip, but one should remember that looking quickly can be a mistake. Even after a week's trip, visitors have barely an introduction to Anza-Borrego country.

Rainfall averages less than 5 inches annually, and the temperature rises toward limits of plant and animal endurance on summer afternoons. Such conditions produce a milieu different from any through which Pacific Crest Trail hikers travel, even different from the Mojave Desert, through which they pass farther north.

Convolutions of broken and folded rock outcrops give the impression of a world turned on end, and the badlands—called "distorted surfaces" on topographic maps—are so sharply etched by wind and occasional running water that they are both picturesque and seemingly forbidding.

But far from being barren, the park has mesquite that forms a "desert jungle," forests of century plants, palms at rocky oases, and enigmatic elephant trees. Our most lasting recollection is not of aridity or "hostility," but of a spindly ocotillo silhouetted against the incandescent lava-red of dawn.

Sunrise and sunset are the best times to be roving these desert ranges. The shadows are longer, providing the landscape with a striking relief, and birds and mammals seem to materialize miraculously, especially around remote and hidden springs. Life is well adapted to this environment, and it is a continuous source of surprise to discover that evolution has managed such successes as leafless plants, animals that drink no water, and seeds that may not sprout for years.

The visitor who is something of a history buff will be amazed at how long human beings have lived in Anza-Borrego country, and how they have adapted to the desert's rigors. There are prehistoric Indian sites, pictographs, historic trail routes, and old stage stations, suggesting that the desert has been occupied, off and on, for as long as there have been human beings.

With so many aspects of interest, one could spend weeks following roads and trails to out-of-the-way places. Good campgrounds, accommodations, exhibits, guidebooks, and informational publications are available.

Ocotillo at sunrise, Anza-Borrego Desert State Park

Beyond Anza-Borrego country rests the Salton Sea, set in the 2,000-square-mile Salton Trough, largest terrestrial area below sea level in the Western Hemisphere.

Northwest along the edge of the Laguna Mountains the Pacific Crest Trail descends through groves of bent oak, where acrobatic ravens twist and turn and dive. Over this terrain pack animals carried the first mail between San Antonio, Texas, and San Diego, California, back in 1857, an operation known as the "Jackass Mail."

This is also Indian territory, and has been for centuries. In fact, a lot of travel has gone over and along these mountains, and present-day hiking here is simply a continuation of the long-prevailing style of human locomotion.

There were innumerable trails throughout southern California long before the Pacific Crest Trail was ever thought of. Wild animals made paths that early Indians followed, and a few became well-traveled routes. Thus, the first European explorers found trails rather well laid out and tested. An exception was Portolá's expedition overland from Mission Velicatá in Baja California to San Diego, the so-called El Camino Real (Royal Highway); this was the only important route blazed through the old West that followed neither a stream course nor an ancient Indian trail.

Early Spanish explorers such as Portolá, Rivera, and Anza were military men, but they had with them men of the church, including Fathers Serra and Garcés, who wanted to raise the cross where the military raised the flag.

Moving northward, the Spaniards established missions and settlements, brought in horses, cattle, and seeds to establish agriculture where little or none existed, and incorporated the native peoples into their work—even if they had to flog them to get them to obey. The Spaniards treated Indians as childlike wards, yet tended to absorb them into their society rather than reject and exterminate them, as the Americans did later.

Eventually, however, relations between the Spaniards and Indians deteriorated. Deception, mistrust, treachery, massacre . . . the natives had little chance in one-sided battles with armed invaders. Those who hid out in the mountains—fugitives in their own land—had some hope of living a little longer and a little freer than their mission-oriented counterparts. Even so, their self-reliance ebbed.

The Indians had been a long time building up that self-reliance. The natural resources and gentle climate of California have always attracted human settlers, somewhat as they appeal to hikers and wilderness users today. In pre-Columbian times this region had one of the largest aboriginal populations north of Mexico; at the beginning of the Spanish conquest, California's Indian population stood at nearly 150,000. These people were not organized into a nation or even a series of communities but rather split into some 500 "tribe-lets" belonging to an estimated 100 dialect groups.

Southern California Indians were not farmers originally; they ate acorns, pine nuts, and other natural foods. They prized and guarded the eagle, whose feathers ornamented ritual costumes, but by and large their lives remained essentially simple, their behavior based on hospitality. Thus they were ill prepared to deal with strangers who lusted for gold and power or who wanted to substitute a new religion for the one they already had.

At California's missions, established in 1769 and after, the Indians living in de facto slavery came to be known as "Mission Indians," and many succumbed to diseases and hopelessness.

Sierra Nevada Indians fared somewhat better. In northern California, a region less hospitable to the newcomers, native tribes remained intact a while longer. But the aborigines could not hold out forever against war, superior arms, broken treaties, and the pressures of invasion. By 1890 their population had declined to 17,000.

Today more than eleven small reservations and rancherias exist in California, though only about 7,000 Indians actually reside on them. In the southern part of the state, several reservations lie near the Pacific Crest Trail, including the Campo, Cuyapaipe, Santa Ysabel, Los Coyotes, Cahuilla, and Morongo.

The principal inhabitants of Indian origin in this region at the southern end of the trail are referred to as Diegueños, and in a mixture of nationalities such as that of present-day California, a newcomer might be hard put to distinguish Diegueños from other citizens. However, their original heritage and culture is in some measure preserved at Cuyamaca Rancho State Park, through which the Pacific Crest Trail passes.

At park headquarters may be seen exhibits of Diegueño culture and history, and the rest of the park's 20,735 acres preserves mountain meadows, canyons, and forests that the early Diegueños knew; in fact, their descendants still come to collect acorns. Seventy-five miles of trails in the park provide an opportunity for walking trips to scenic viewpoints, mountain summits, and historic sites.

Long before the Jackass Mail, Spanish explorers, and Indian tribes, there were well-adapted residents who managed to survive, at least in some degree, the human wars and invasions. These were wild animals, and it is as possible now to have sudden surprise encounters with them as it was during Indian days.

We arose one morning and went out on the trail as the first faint trace of dawn began to appear. Suddenly we saw an owl perched in an old oak over the trail, silhouetted against the eastern sky. It was barely visible in the darkness, but we could see its head turn one way and remain motionless for a while, then turn in another di-

Coulter pine cone

rection. Eventually the bird flew out across a grassy swale that had probably been its hunting ground during the night and disappeared into the woods on the other side.

Not far north of Cuyamaca Rancho, hikers who are interested in early mining days can delay their travels in the mountain town of Julian, where gold and gunplay once constituted the milieu of miners. Between 1869 and 1880, four to five million dollars in gold were taken from mines around Julian and hauled down Banner Grade toward the Anza-Borrego Desert.

A stamp mill went up, saloons appeared, Julian boomed. But inevitably the dream burst, and the miners went to Tombstone, over the horizon eastward in Arizona. The old mines remain, and Julian, now less raw, has become a mountain community in the heart of orchard and cattle country. One old mine has been restored to working order, and a museum recalls the days of buckboards and ore carts.

Beyond Julian and Banner Canyon, the Pacific Crest Trail moves north through broken granite terrain and semidesert vegetation. We pass sandy washes filled with willows and live oaks and skirt the rolling hills of rich green agricultural lands, but this is only a brief interlude, for the route leads back into jumbles of boulders and up into granite mountains again.

Sometimes the companions one picks up along the trail seem surprising: roses, thousands of them. Not the conventional garden species but a rose-family tree with peeling, shaggy, stringy, russet bark. This is red shanks, which grows in almost pure forests at certain places in southern California.

Visible 10 miles to the west are the shining domes of the famed observatory atop Mount Palomar, well worth a side trip. Part of the Hale Observatories, owned by the California Institute of Technology and operated jointly with the Carnegie Institute of Washington, D.C., the Palomar Observatory has been functioning since 1948. The big Hale telescope, with its 200-inch mirror, weighs 530 tons and reaches well over a billion light years into space.

Near the observatory lies Palomar Mountain State Park, a 1,886-acre ridgetop reserve of cool, fern-lined ravines and deep forests of pine, fir, and cedar. Adjacent to that park, the Agua Tibia Wilderness of nearly 26,000 acres contains natural ecosystems that have miraculously escaped fires for more than a century. Public access is restricted during most of the summer fire-danger period because of the necessity of protecting the fragile forest from careless campers and smokers. Once in, however, hikers can observe ceanothus, red shanks, and manzanita of unusually large dimensions.

Coming to the San Jacinto Mountains, the hiker experiences one of the highest and most rapid rises on the Pacific Crest Trail, followed

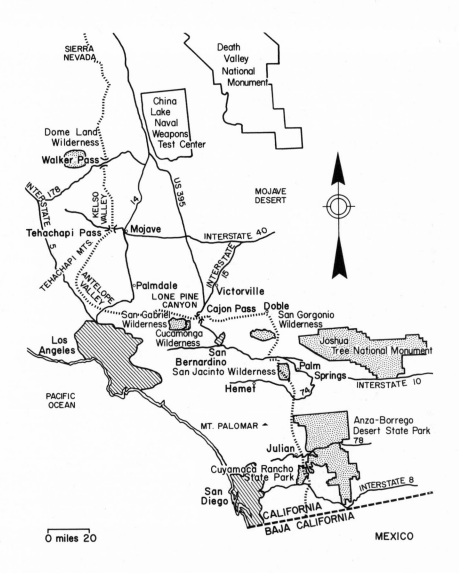

THE PACIFIC CREST TRAIL IN SOUTHERN CALIFORNIA

by one of the steepest plunges in any mountain range this side of Alaska.

From Coyote Canyon, at about 3,000 feet, to the summit of San Jacinto Peak is a straight-line distance of 25 miles and a rise of 7,800 feet. On the north side, down the face of the San Jacinto Mountains to San Gorgonio Pass, within a horizontal distance of 6 miles, the elevation falls nearly 10,000 feet.

Ascending this vast desert massif, the traveler finds that nature, despite occasional violent phases, arranges biological systems in a rather orderly manner. Vegetation encircles the mountains in over-lapping bands of cactus, chaparral, juniper, pine, and fir, depending on temperature of exposure. Likewise, the fauna varies from roadrun-ners to mountain lions.

This is an oversimplification, but each ecosystem is clearly responsive to temperature and moisture, and for hikers the pattern of changes in vegetation up and down the mountains becomes quite predictable. Even the variations can be predicted: on sunny slopes one hikes through desertlike environments, and in shady ravines among species of upper mountain plants. Such intermingling might seem of interest only to an ecologist, but hikers living with it mile after mile begin to gain new insights into this order of plant dis-tribution. And besides, they have a vested interest in cool spots, shade, and springs.

The long-distance hiker will take this climb in stride, but less hardy travelers may be troubled by strenuous hiking at high alti-tude. However, those who cannot make the ascent on foot need not be deprived of the beauties of the San Jacintos, for these summits are among the more accessible along the Pacific Crest Trail. On the east side of the mountains the Palm Springs Aerial Tramway rises to the edge of Mount San Jacinto Wilderness State Park. On the west, California State Route 243 winds in and out among ridges and canyons.

The high country is an island of solitude. The state park is literally a wilderness within a wilderness, surrounded by the fed-erally administered San Jacinto Wilderness, part of San Bernardino National Forest. The Pacific Crest Trail goes through both areas and is presided over by stately Jeffrey pines. As early as November the summits may be buried hip-deep in snow, which enhances the con-trast of red pine bark and clear blue sky.

The State of California's wilderness park here contains 13,521 acres, and because it is so popular, which could lead to damaging overuse, park authorities limit the size of visiting groups. There are also rules designed to keep the wilderness clean, quiet, and intact, and would-be travelers should check in at the boundary ranger station not far from the tramway terminal.

As for the federal area, consisting of nearly 22,000 acres, week-end hikes have been attractive adjuncts to Pacific Crest Trail use, but, alas, the place also became too popular for its own good. Since 1971, wilderness use permits have been required, and the public demand has far exceeded the capacity of this relatively small and fragile area. Consequently, the U.S. Forest Service controls the num-ber of wilderness campers—and may have other regulations in effect from time to time.

Thus, as in all wilderness areas along the Pacific Crest Trail, hikers should obtain permits before entering. (See mailing addresses, Appendix 2.) The long-distance hiker who plans to enter more than one wilderness and camp overnight should play safe and obtain a permit for each area along the route. This means that a definite itinerary and time schedule should be prepared in advance.

The east face of the San Jacinto Mountains shows how the Penin-sular Ranges have been broken and raised into high sheer faces. Ascending or descending by cable car from Palm Springs, the visi-tor swings past cliff faces that have been thoroughly fractured and the cracks filled with younger rock of lighter shades. The result is an extraordinary diagrammatic pattern of igneous dikes and sills.

The lifting and fracturing of this eastern face, as well as the multitude of cliffs on the rest of the mountain, testify as to the instability of the earth's crust in this region. Along the San Jacinto and Elsinore fault zones the Peninsular Ranges have been severely ripped asunder by primeval earth forces and thrust upward, inch by inch. The hiker may feel no movement underfoot and the rocks may seem as solid as ever. But the land has obviously been lifted far faster than erosion could wear it down. Along those faults move-ment takes place more or less continuously and imperceptibly be-neath the forest floor, and even though the hiker detects no motion, the whole character of the Peninsular Ranges is based on faulting.

The same is true of the route ahead. For the next 1,000 miles the Pacific Crest Trail follows some of the most active fault zones in the world. At the moment, however, it is well to enjoy these tranquil mountains while we can, for the prospect of going north now becomes rather painful. We must descend from the San Jacintos into San Gorgonio Pass, through which men hurl themselves and their machines at a frenzied pace. We must go down from pine-scented mountain breezes into polluted air rising up out of the Los Angeles Basin. We cross an interstate highway and railroad tracks and go under transmission lines. And, long before reaching the pass, we hear the ceaseless roar of trucks and cars.

Through all this we try to find some fragment of wild nature to engrave in our minds and sustain us across the pass back up into the mountains on the opposite side. It needn't be much, just some-thing to hold onto, something to remind us of reality.

Not far back, we had glimpsed, through the pines, a face colored yellow, red, white, and black, as though some shrunken clown were jumping around and playing tricks. It was an acorn woodpecker, flying up to the trunk of an old pine and clinging there. It delivered a short chatter and then, in a flutter of feathers and flash of white, flew away. The color, the eyes, the echoes of its voice remained imprinted in a sequence of images that could be carried across to the San Bernardino Mountains. Some persons may regard that fleeting image as a slender reed against the tyranny of industrialization, but with the memory of this bird we could fight every vehicle on Interstate 10.

Rabbit brush, Lone Pine Canyon

3

Transverse Ranges

Men so much love noise and stir . . . ;
the pleasure of solitude is a thing incompre-
hensible.

Blaise Pascal, *Pensées*, 1670

FROM SAN GORGONIO PASS the Pacific Crest Trail goes up Whitewater
Canyon, which could as well be called White Rock Canyon. This
gleaming terrain is the last of low semiarid environments for a while,
and we pause to examine one of its principal attractions: the desert
willow.

This tree is no willow, but rather a member of the bignonia
family. Its long leaves and predilection for moist places give it a
willow aspect, but true willows never had flowers like this. The
blossoms are orchidlike, white and lavender and intricately designed.
They appear to be out of place where creosote bush and catclaw
predominate, but on the contrary, these plants have adapted, and
Southwest deserts would be incomplete without them. The flowers
may be seen from May to September, and if anyone thinks the
Pacific Crest Trail is without wild gardens, even where it goes through
hot, dry canyons, the desert willow dispels such doubts.

The Peninsular Ranges, which brought us north by northwest
from Mexico, now lie behind, and we enter an entirely new physio-
graphic province. Trending mostly west, the mountains ahead lie
transverse to the general run of California ranges, and so are called
Transverse Ranges. They include the San Bernardinos, San Gabriels,
and San Rafaels and are the dividing line between northern and
southern California. These mountains extend westward past Santa
Barbara, literally into the sea; the Channel Islands are believed to be
summits of sunken and submerged sections of the Transverse Ranges.

We start climbing. The heat and our perspiration now seem oppressive. The eastern part of the Transverse Ranges is made up mostly of igneous and metamorphic rocks, some as old as 1.7 billion years. The western part contains more sedimentary beds and thus exhibits layers, including folded strata. Faults exist throughout, not surprising in a region where the earth's crust is so active. In certain places these breaks in the rock determine the configuration of the landscape, because streams along fault lines have cut canyons and valleys. The east and west forks of the San Gabriel River are examples.

Each year's precipitation in these mountains averages 30 inches, while out in the desert it is scarcely a tenth of that. Much precipitation falls between December and April, mostly in a few severe storms, with summers usually dry. Under these circumstances, the San Gabriel and San Bernardino Mountains have no large permanent streams, a point all hikers should remember.

From a distance the San Bernardino Mountains, a faulted granite mass with signs of glaciation, look like the prow of a giant ship sailing into the desert. To starboard, 10 miles east of the Pacific Crest Trail, lies Joshua Tree National Monument, a vast desert reserve accessible by road and trail. There are immense collections of quartz-monzonite boulders in the Monument, rivaling the terrain down along the Mexican boundary. But Joshua Tree has less chaparral and more cactus—gardens of cholla on gently descending pediments, and Joshua trees themselves, sharp-pointed yuccas that reach 30 feet in height. We shall see more of this bizarre plant near the Tehachapi Mountains, where the Pacific Crest Trail passes through miles of it.

Into the San Bernardinos the trail ascends through piñon-juniper woodland. Desert vegetation gradually diminishes. Getting to the summit of 11,502-foot San Gorgonio Mountain is a side trip, for the Pacific Crest Trail goes only around the flank of the peak. Notwithstanding the abundance of winter snow, there may be little water in this region, especially in mid and late summer, so hikers should consult a trail guidebook and local authorities.

The views remain striking all the way around the prow of the mountains; there are especially dramatic panoramas of the Mojave Desert, with its miles of creosote bush. All this, together with deep blue sky and the fragrance of pines, may find the hiker lamenting that eighty years on earth will not be enough . . . nor ninety . . . nor a hundred.

One tries to sort these scenes and sounds, but how is it possible? The music of the wind. Stream beds strewn with white boulders of granite and gneiss. Cool shadows of sycamores, willows, cottonwoods. Tall orange trunks of pine. Twisted oaks, like dancers with a hundred arms. Chaparral enclosing the trail. Jays dashing through thickets. Ravines. Canyons. Cliffs. . . .

Joshua tree at sunset, Joshua Tree National Monument

And miles of manzanita. One might as well call these the Manzanita Mountains. This hardy heather with the tough green leaves puts up effective barriers to off-trail travel. Not that it possesses thorns; its branches are so numerous they tangle the legs and feet. The branches possess a handsome maroon bark that shines as though some high-gloss polish had been applied. In spring the minute flowers hang like clusters of silent pink bells. Few plants are as widely distributed along the Pacific Crest Trail. This *Arctostaphylos,* Latin for "bearberry," is fire-resistant and drought-resistant, and heralds a tough natural tenacity that allows it to grow from low elevations to high.

The traveler fond of wild foods may have the good fortune to be along this section of trail when cones of piñon pine mature. The seeds are sweet, delicious, and good eating, but it will take some luck to find them because of keen competition with birds and squirrels. Early Indians solved this problem by gathering the cones just before they ripened and putting them around a fire. The heat dried out the cones and ejected toasted seeds.

Our route goes through miles of piñon-juniper country on the middle-elevation flanks of the San Bernardino Mountains. Piñons are relatively small and slow-growing; trees less than 30 feet tall can be more than two hundred years old. They thrive on arid slopes, and in August may be fully loaded with dark brown cones.

For touches of art and sculpture, one turns to junipers: weather-beaten, twisted, stocky, gnarled, cinnamon-brown on the trunk, gray-green in the leaves, bluish white in the berrylike cones. Sometimes they stand alone in sheltered vales and grow symmetrically, but that seems rare. The more common convolutions challenge a photographer, who will find more grotesque designs and contorted growth forms than there will ever be time to focus on.

So one selects . . . and goes on.

The trail now heads generally west, withdraws somewhat from the desert environment, and occasionally touches sylvan settings of incense cedar, oak, pine, and clear running streams. Water may be only a temporary part of the environment, however, because in summer the sources diminish or dry up.

Suddenly we are in gold country again. Little remains of the old mining camp of Doble, and after another year's erosion a little less will remain. On the peaceful meadows of Holcomb Valley we must use our imagination to bring back the mining communities, Two-Gun Bill's saloon, toll roads, prospectors, Southern sympathizers, secessionists, hangman's trees, and other elements of the 1860s gold rush. The only remnants are a few crumbling cabins and, somewhere, unmarked graves where the nearly forgotten people of those towns, those fights, those mines, are returning to dust.

Mount San Gorgonio

Unfortunately, at present the Pacific Crest Trail in the San Bernardino Mountains must sometimes thread its way through the kinds of environments hikers try to get away from: summer homes, garages, gas stations, theaters, shopping centers, resorts, rifle ranges, ski tows. At certain scenic mountain lakes, trailers lie parked side by side and transmission towers march across the landscape. When it is ultimately completed, the Pacific Crest Trail will avoid such accoutrements of civilization; however, unless the power lines are buried, the views of them will remain.

Though dense human populations result in mountains checkered with private roads and ornamented with No Trespassing signs, this is not as worrisome as the long-distance destruction of forests by air pollutants. Untreated residue from human consumption of energy has frequently filled the Los Angeles Basin to overflowing, with disastrous effects upon forests of the surrounding Peninsular and Transverse Ranges.

Photochemical smog, filtering into the forests and across mountain ranges, has left widespread destruction. Ozone in the smog produces a yellowish mottled effect on ponderosa pine needles, causing them to drop and thus killing the branches from the bottom of the tree upward. This has occurred as far as 80 miles east of Los Angeles. Aerial surveys in 1969 in San Bernardino National Forest showed thousands of acres heavily damaged. An estimated 1,298,000 trees were affected, 82 percent moderately, 15 percent severely, and 3 percent killed. Trees that did not die from oxidant injury became prey for pine bark beetles.

In a publication of the University of California Statewide Air Pollution Center, Dr. Paul R. Miller, a plant pathologist with the U.S. Forest Service, said, "There is no known method for restoring the health of smog-damaged trees—short of placing them in a filtered air enclosure. Prevention of air pollution at its sources is the only real cure. . . ."

The forest has enough problems of its own, what with wind, hail, and lightning. The hiker will find plentiful evidence of fire, as in mountain ravines where black snags of pines remain from past conflagrations, or in chaparral country, where new oaks grow from old blackened stumps.

At Cajon Pass, the trail proceeds northwestward above Lone Pine Canyon into the San Gabriel Mountains. At the pass may be seen sedimentary rock layers tilted as though they were gates to some drunken drama in an upended world. That is not far wrong. The San Gabriels, once called the Sierra Madre, consist of crystalline metamorphic and granitic blocks 60 miles long and up to 20 miles wide, eroded into deep canyons that lead up to sharp crests. One authority says that this range has been faulted as intensively as any other mountain region in the world. Lone Pine Canyon is a suspiciously straight-line depression, almost unbending for perhaps 20 miles. That signals a fault zone where plate blocks of the earth's crust have broken and slipped alongside each other. Actually, the rift of which it is a part extends for hundreds of miles ahead of and behind us.

We are walking on the famous, and death-dealing, San Andreas fault.

The rock crust of California is riven with giant fractures. Like other land masses around the Pacific Basin, this region is subject to adjustments in the vast plates that make up the earth's surface. That these plates should shift and slide and break under the enormous strains of an evolving earth is not surprising. Such breaks, or faults, are readily visible as long rips in the landscape: straight canyons, truncated ridges, and offset creeks. They are even manifested by disrupted fences, roads, and railroad tracks.

Master of all is the San Andreas fault, which extends from the Gulf of California region to Point Reyes, north of San Francisco, and on under the Pacific Ocean. The fault is at least 600 miles long and 20 miles deep.

Perhaps the most amazing phenomenon is how far the rocks on one side have moved horizontally with respect to those on the other: some 350 miles. At an average rate of 2 inches or so a year, this much offset represents a considerable amount of time; the fault is estimated to have been in existence for 100 million years.

In all that time, sudden breaks and slippages have shaken the land no telling how many times. The largest known earthquakes resulting from disruptions along this fault occurred in 1838, 1857, and 1906—the latter causing 700 deaths and millions of dollars in property damage. The next big tremor could produce disaster figures of astronomical proportions.

The fault line is not a dramatic bold escarpment, and hikers will seldom be able to identify it from the ground. The rift zone, measuring from a few feet to a mile wide, is best seen from mountains above, or from the air. But at least hikers can determine from maps and trail guides when they are walking on it. Lone Pine Canyon, apart from its telltale straightness, looks like most other chaparral-covered valleys, and one might not guess that beneath it are some of the most powerful forces on earth, waiting to be unleashed.

Apparently they are unleashed, bit by bit. Where the hills in this region are composed of relatively unstable sediments, the soil occasionally collapses and slides down into a valley. Vegetation covers these slumps in due course, but the outlines still reveal what happened.

Will an earthquake strike while we walk on the fault? This ques-

Seed pods on yucca stalk

tion may cause trepidation in some persons, but we should bear in mind that hiking out here on the fault zone is probably safer than walking the streets of cities or driving on country roads.

Should we feel a thud or shock, then swaying or rolling motions, we can regard it as exceptionally good fortune. If no stones fall on us, or if we otherwise sustain no injury, we should enjoy every moment of such a rare event. Releases of tremendous energy are felt by few people in the wilds, and the phenomenon of a strong earthquake is so uncommon that chances of experiencing one are slim.

We see houses, even mountain communities (Wrightwood, for example) built right on the fault zone and wonder if the owners knew what they were doing. The answer is likely that they did; the San Andreas fault is a well-known geologic feature.

Indeed, there have been pitched battles between scientists, who would like to keep the rift zone and associated unstable areas free of settlement for safety reasons, and real estate developers, who would like to see widespread construction projects under way. The builders have frequently won, and the number of schools and hospitals constructed along the rift zone seems unbelievable. One engineer says that you can trace the San Andreas fault by following the line of schools built on it.

As for placing one's home on the zone, what must residents who build and stay in so potentially dangerous a region think? Mostly they react as people do in hurricane and tornado country: what will be will be. If disaster comes they will rebuild and go on. It is nature's way. It is God's will.

To a hiker the energies of earthquakes are something to marvel at, but many people, perhaps most, do not see it quite that way. They may regard tremors with fear, dread, and anxiety. Charles Darwin pointed out that nothing was quite so unstable as the level of the crust of the earth, and that one second of time during an earthquake would be sufficient to create in some persons a tremendous insecurity that hours of reflection would not have produced. But the informed hiker knows that earthquakes are simply landscape adjustments on a restless earth. Attuned to little miracles, walkers are readily able to appreciate big ones.

After a while the Pacific Crest Trail climbs up out of the San Andreas rift zone and into pine and fir country again, this time along the Angeles Crest.

About 3 miles by trail to the south is the Cucamonga Wilderness, the northern edge of which is the highest point in the San Gabriel range, Mount San Antonio (Mount Baldy), 10,064 feet. It is one of the last remaining habitats for bighorn sheep in southern California.

Then for 10 miles or so the route passes along the northern

boundary of the San Gabriel Wilderness. Hikers who wish to divert into this wilderness for a while do so at their own risk and peril. Few trails enter the preserve, the cross-country exploration is principally over rugged terrain, with sharp ledges, sheer rock faces, deep canyons filled with immense boulders, and tough shrubbery laced with vicious mountain whitethorn. Travelers with a desire to test their endurance in a rough mountain environment ought to get their fill of it here. In fact, they should go with someone rather than alone, for reasons of safety and possible rescue. The U.S. Forest Service prefers that persons off-trail in rugged country travel in fours; moreover, some members of the party should have rescue training and rock-climbing experience.

A less exacting side trip is up to the summit of Mount Baden-Powell, elevation 9,399 feet, where limber pines more than a thousand years old still grow. In addition, there are numerous trails and mountain roads throughout the Angeles National Forest that offer access to hidden places.

The San Gabriels are full of legends, Indian lore, Gold Rush history, and deep canyons. Trails lead past old mines and townsites, waterfalls, and spectacular overlooks, and to the Mount Wilson astronomical observatory, which has exhibits and a visitor's gallery. Some trails are indistinct and nonmaintained and should be traveled with care. Others enter parts of the forest that are closed during periods of high fire danger in summer. Some places have sheer drop-offs of hundreds of feet and are too often the scene of fatalities. The San Gabriels are not foothills; they are rugged mountains.

As the Pacific Crest Trail comes down out of them via the Mill Creek Summit, in relatively remote terrain, it is hard to believe that we are closer to large cities than at any other point on the Trail. Beyond the intervening ridges to the south, in a direct line of about 15 miles, lie Hollywood, Burbank, Glendale, Pasadena, and other communities in the Los Angeles Basin.

The mountains shield us from noise and screen out the sometimes frenetic pace of urban life, although we do not escape the city entirely. Shifting breezes carry pollutants high above the ranges and at times obscure the canyon and desert views on this side. Nevertheless, the mountain greenery freshens our air. We make the best of what we have and, grateful for the quiet, hike ahead.

Past granite outcrops, shattered cliffs, manzanita, mountain mahogany, deer, acorn woodpeckers, and the aroma of sagebrush, the traveler drops again into chaparral country. The trees all but disappear, surviving only in sheltered ridgetop ravines or along stream canyons. Scrub oak, yucca, and the highly flammable chamise dominate.

Given the right combination of atmospheric conditions, lightning, or human carelessness, chaparral can explode into intense and

Yucca leaves

rapidly spreading fire. Beneath the shrubbery can be seen tremendous quantities of dry chaff—old buckwheat and rabbit brush, for example —and there are dead and fallen yuccas, light as a feather and consumed like tissue paper in a campfire.

To some people these wildfires should be stopped at all costs. But chaparral evolved as a fire-susceptible community partly because of the long period of unrelieved dryness to which the dense bush forest is subjected each spring and summer. The situation becomes acute when winds and temperatures are high and there is little fog. This leaves the vegetation tinder-dry.

For as long as men can remember, and for perhaps 2 million years before that, there have been sweeping and intensely hot brush fires in these natural communities.

But the chaparral, though leveled, makes a remarkable comeback. Chamise, the most common species, sprouts quickly after a fire. Its seeds and the seeds of other plants germinate readily in the rich ashes. Latent buds below ground sprout and send up tender shoots that are palatable to deer.

Fire thus seems to be a beneficial pruning process in nature's economy. Where fires have been artificially suppressed, the plant debris may accumulate to 40 tons per acre. Under such circumstances a fire, once started, quickly becomes a holocaust that is very difficult and hazardous to control.

However fierce the fire, though, plants make a comeback when people leave them alone. Human beings assumed that fire was bad and so launched immense and costly campaigns against it, including extensive fuel breaks. But fire and chaparral have long existed in harmony, and chaparral is an outstanding example of fire-type vegetation. In this respect, it is like that of the Florida Everglades or the Sierra big trees.

Scientists think that the policy of excluding fire should be reconsidered, and they recommend the burning of certain sections of chaparral at certain times, perhaps over cycles of several years. However, given man's penchant for building homes in chaparral domain, it would be neccessary to establish fuel breaks, or some kind of buffer zones, where the fire could not get out of control. Also, some people feel that prescribed burning would be another artificial manipulation of the environment.

Such conflicting pressures have existed for years. Range managers want to eradicate chaparral so that more grass will grow for cattle. Fire control officers want it removed on account of the fire hazard. Conservationists want it kept intact. And soil experts view it as splendid erosion control.

Those hiking through miles of wild chaparral take few off-trail excursions because the underbrush is virtually impenetrable: woody, rigid, interlocked. Anyone who doesn't think so is welcome to try a few miles of dense chaparral "plowing" and see what happens to clothes and unprotected skin.

On a quiet day it is difficult to imagine how fires can sweep across these hills with such devastation. But the hiker on a ridgetop during high winds will understand. Gale power can decidedly limit progress along the trail. The wind comes in at upward of 50 miles an hour, approaching hurricane force. It takes away our breath, pushes us back, or bowls us over. There simply is no point in going on against such odds—which are even worse if, as in winter, the temperature is low and the result is a chill factor that could be dangerous to hikers ill prepared and caught in the open.

By contrast, there are some delightful sheltered places along this portion of the trail, and refuge can be found in these. Hikers may search for secluded sites in canyons that cut across the hills or may stay in deep ravines roofed over with ceanothus, cherry, and oak. Or they can relax on sunny grass slopes protected from the wind. However, they had better be able to identify and avoid poison oak if they want this interlude to remain idyllic.

Let the winds roar over the ridges. Down here we are too busy to care. Clean water flows through crystal sands of granitic quartz and feldspar. Flocks of quail fly up and shatter the quiet. At lower elevations we meet old friends, such as the digger pine, that familiar tree with multiple trunks and a sparse supply of needles.

Continuing along the San Andreas rift zone, the trail parallels Antelope Valley, which is well settled and farmed but does have notable wildflower displays—especially poppies and paintbrush—and several small wildflower sanctuaries. History buffs will find themselves lingering in the valley if they start searching for old Indian campsites and abandoned mines. However, they should avoid non-maintained shafts for safety reasons, and instead find an old display mine that has been shored up, lighted, and opened to the public.

At the western end of Antelope Valley the Pacific Crest Trail turns abruptly at right angles, crosses the San Andreas fault for the last time, and heads northeast along another fault, the Garlock.

The proposed route of the trail leads up onto the crest of the Tehachapi Mountains at about 6,000 feet elevation, but at this writing, problems of private property prevent a hiker's passage. So one must follow a temporary route at a lower elevation of about 4,000 feet, where the heat and dust of the desert in July and August are oppressive. This means that drinking water in canteen or pack becomes something more than a luxury. A traveler may choose to hike at night in order to conserve moisture and avoid the heat, but should have sturdy boots as a defense against rattlesnakes and be certain of a well-defined trail that can be followed in the dark.

The Garlock fault stretches more than 150 miles from Tejon Pass to Death Valley. The Tehachapi Mountain uplift, one bold fea-

Joshua tree forest, Tehachapi Pass

ture along it, is topped by Double Mountain at 7,988 feet elevation. This massif is granitic, with metamorphic rocks such as marble. On the northern side of Tehachapi Pass, farther on, the Garlock fault constitutes the southern boundary of the Sierra Nevada.

The fracture line, in reality a zone of many parallel breaks, is marked by small canyons and escarpments, and there is evidence of slow creeping along it. For example, roads over it develop cracks shortly after being paved, a manifestation of forces shearing and pulling apart the blocks of rock beneath.

To the east, the Mojave Desert covers thousands of square miles. Throughout much of it the indomitable creosote bush prevails, but the most dramatic plant is clearly the Joshua tree. To some observers this member of the lily family is simply the strangest tree in North America. It seems less a tree than a collection of daggers; the foot-long leaves are rigid, sharp-pointed, and edged with sawteeth. Few desert plants, cactus included, are quite as formidable, and most animals, including human beings, stay away from it. But the Joshua tree is vulnerable to animals that burrow within, and dead or alive, it provides a home for organisms such as pack rats and night lizards. It also provides a perching and nesting spot for desert birds, certainly a safe place to raise a family.

The interdependent relationship of yucca plants with yucca moths, which lay eggs in the flowers so that larvae can have food and in the process pollinate the flowers, is one of the most classic examples of ecological cooperation.

The shapes of this asymmetrical tree are infinite, and at sunset the silhouette is ghostlike. Arms may rise, outstretch, or dangle, as though some prophetic Joshua were leading his legions into a promised land. Such is one theory of how the plant came to be named by early Mormon travelers.

Other explorers were not so impressed. When John C. Frémont crossed Tehachapi Pass and moved into groves of them, he found their "stiff and ungraceful forms" no help to his party and called the Joshua tree "the most repulsive tree in the vegetable kingdom." Nevertheless, the handsome leathery greenish flowers, plus carpets of poppy and verbena that grow beneath them, give the Joshua tree forest a unique beauty. And no two trees have the same contortions. Walking among them, our eyes are constantly roving over the grotesque shapes and forms, and we find ourselves almost as strangers in a strange land.

Concentrations of Joshua trees persist up into the foothills of the Tehachapi Mountains, to Tehachapi Pass, and northward to the very skirts of the Sierra Nevada. On moonlit nights these plants resemble nothing less than armies of spiny goblins, arms askew, trying to climb the mountains toward some celestial perdition.

Ponderosa pine bark

4

Into the Sierra

In the beginning the world was rock.

Northern Miwok creation myth

NORTH OF TEHACHAPI PASS the Pacific Crest Trail enters the Sierra Nevada and heads into high country again, rising out of the desert. But the desert is never very far away, framed by either piñon pines or digger pines or both. Sometimes it is simply a bright blur of dust or smog, and even on clear days the distances are so great that few details can be detected on the far horizons.

·Yet out there, spread across thousands of square miles, is virtually every enterprise men have contrived in the past century, from borax mines to rocket propulsion scaffolds.

Edwards Air Force Base, the nation's second largest, is a center for testing new aircraft, so a hiker shouldn't be surprised to see odd shapes flying over, perceive unfamiliar lights, or hear roaring sounds in the distance. These serve to remind us of man's temporary technology and give us a fresh appreciation of nature's stability and durability.

Northwest of the town of Inyokern is the sprawling Naval Weapons Center, established in late 1943 to undertake a crash effort in rocket testing and development. At that site were spawned the Shrike, Sidewinder, Walleye, and Zuñi missiles.

The contrasts and parallels are inescapable: there on the desert floor man's development of lethal systems; up here wild animals also with lethal systems. One is reminded that defense and aggression are acts of natural law, and therefore proper for human beings and wild beasts; but on this trail we are inclined to be optimistic that Homo sapiens will someday perfect the skills of managing lives without taking them.

Out in the desert are colorful canyons where motion pictures have been filmed, and where devotees of motorcycles camp and run their hilly routes. On holidays, cyclists and dune buggy aficionados come by the hundreds to Jawbone Canyon, and on the rounded slopes leave their tracks and grooves for posterity. In this arid climate, a great deal of posterity will be able to observe the results.

Some canyons are rich in the fossil remains of vertebrate animals such as camels, rhinos, and mastodons. Gold was once mined there, and some places have been attractive to rock hounds because of their quartz minerals, including agate.

Speaking of fossils, the mountains, canyons, and deserts in this region possess remarkable remnants of long-vanished ecosystems. Such fossils are rather a rarity along the Pacific Crest Trail because most rocks from here to the north are either granite or lava, which were once molten and thus essentially devoid of organisms.

But here in ancient times were environments notably favorable to life—green meadows, lush prairies, lakes, marshes, and rivers. From fossils recovered, it is clear that primeval landscapes in southern California were populated with ichthyosaurs (fishlike reptiles), crocodiles, rhinoceroses, tapirs, sloths, mastodons, camels, saber-toothed cats, and dog-bears.

Ancestors of modern horses lived in subtropical savanna-woodlands where the Tehachapi Mountains are today. In places just below the Pacific Crest Trail are rich assemblages of fossil plants, including petrified wood, though much of the latter has been hauled away by rock dealers.

Today the desert slopes and mountains become awash with wild flowers at the onset of spring. In counterpoint, the foothills are also strewn with remains of old camps, dumps, and debris of human settlement.

For a while the trail continues through different desert environments. Cactuses grow in the hills, and Joshua trees seem to pour through the passes.

As we rise, the contrast with what we left becomes more marked. Up here it is cool; down there it is often hot. Up here it is wet and much of the year snowy; down there the annual precipitation may be only a few inches. Up here grows rich vegetation; down there lie plains with sparsely scattered brush.

The Sierra Nevada is directly responsible for the perpetual drought down there because these mountains block the passage of eastbound moisture. Saturated air flowing inland from the Pacific Ocean rises, condenses, and precipitates nearly all of its moisture in the mountains before going over the summit and down the eastern side. That downward passage of air from the mountains can be a formidable event; dry winds descend from cliffs and streak out across the plains, pick up clouds of dust and jagged particles of granite, "frost" car windows, and take the paint off vehicles trying to get through.

From up here on the Pacific Crest Trail we look down over desert valleys that are sometimes inhospitable. Millenniums ago large bodies of water occupied a number of the basins. Those times of greater rainfall are gone, however, and only saline lakes remain. Mono Lake, farther north, lies at the foot of the Sierra Nevada, and the concentric terraces around it depict ancient shorelines of a much larger body of water.

Far beyond, 120 miles to the southeast, is the master basin, Death Valley, nearly 2 million acres of which are preserved as a national monument. Hikers wishing to have a go at trekking between the lowest and highest points in the contiguous 48 states will have to endure some considerable extremes from the 14,494-foot peak of Mount Whitney to the 282 feet below sea level near Badwater.

The Pacific Crest Trail comes to Kelso Valley, one of the most charming vales along the route. It contains dense forests of Joshua trees set amid naked rock formations and fallen boulders. Chamise is still with us. Willows and cottonwoods line the washes. Sagebrush, Mormon tea, and other shrubs mix in from place to place.

At 4,000 feet, Kelso Valley is a high desert basin, rimmed on the east by nearly treeless ridges and on the west by forested uplands dotted with mines. The town of Sageland, born in 1867, catered to miners of the El Dorado District, and though it had stores, saloons, boarding houses, and a stage line, was as ephemeral as the mines and lasted scarcely a dozen years. Some of the mines were operated, if only intermittently, until the 1940s.

Up in the Piute Mountains are numerous abandoned mines. And if one explores there long enough he will also find abandoned cabins, sawmills, roads, and trails.

Something to look for here is the rare Piute cypress. Most cypresses in California grow in limited numbers in secluded locations. The Cuyamaca cypress, on the southwest side of Cuyamaca Peak, is another example near the Pacific Crest Trail. Here in the Piutes, where the woods are dominated by piñon, juniper, oak, and digger pine, the cone-shaped Piute cypress grows in a remote site north of Bald Eagle Peak. When flowering in February and March the trees become dusted with yellow pollen, and the foliage turns rich green. During summer the aspect is a dusty gray-green. But always there is the characteristic fibrous bark that hangs in strips.

Kelso Valley and environs constitute one of the places along the Pacific Crest Trail where hikers can spend days exploring the hidden trails and side roads, remote canyons, Joshua tree forests, and rocky hills. Photographic opportunities are limitless, not only because of panoramic views but also for multiple combinations of boulders and vegetation.

From high points we look to the north and perceive an escarpment unlike anything we have seen before. It is a mass of gray rock rising 4,000 feet from the foot of Kelso Creek. This sudden rise is not as much as that on the north face of the San Jacinto Mountains, but it is the edge of a vast plateau, and the beginning of the Sierra Nevada's central high mountain region.

In a way, the walls of Kelso Valley and rugged ramparts of the Scodie Mountains prepare us for the wilderness to come. Kelso Valley, the South Fork Valley of the Kern River, and Walker Pass contain the last highways, farms, and communities a hiker sees for more than 200 miles north along the Pacific Crest Trail.

There were few communities and no highways at all when Joseph Reddeford Walker's exploring party came through here in 1834. He had traveled to California from the fledgling United States, far to the east across what seemed like endless deserts. He was not the first to cross those deserts, but he had the same problems: aridity, heat, hunger, and hostile Indians (he and his party of trappers massacred more than a score of the latter).

The group crossed the Sierra Nevada at what is now Sonora Pass, descended the Stanislaus River into the San Joaquin Valley, and proceeded to San Francisco Bay. On his return, Walker went south to the vicinity of present-day Bakersfield, turned east and went up the twisting, rock-strewn Kern River Canyon, a prodigious feat in itself. Guided by Indians, he crossed the Sierra at a low point which has been given the name Walker Pass.

Several plaques pay tribute to Walker's "discovery," and the site has been designated a Registered National Historic Landmark by the U.S. Department of the Interior. But Walker did not discover the pass; he was led there. Zenas Leonard, one of the trappers in the party, kept a journal in which he describes meeting a group of Indians on the western side of the mountains:

"We passed one night with these Indians, during which time they informed us of an accessible passage over the mountain. In the morning we resumed our journey, hiring two of these Indians as pilots, to go with us across the mountain."

After some difficulty in getting through snow in the pass, they managed to descend into temperate climate and good forage on the eastern side.

Obviously the Indians were aware of major passes and landmarks. There were certainly plenty of Indians to explore the wilderness. The Sierra Nevada and vicinity was one of the most densely populated parts of North America before the coming of Europeans. The original inhabitants had known the peaks, passes, and forests for years and undoubtedly had names for prominent landmarks.

They lived here for centuries, thousands of them, without, as far as is known, causing the extinction of any animal species, destroying the landscape, or endangering their survival by upsetting naturally balanced ecosystems.

The Indians left little record of their history; ethnologists gather details of their lives and habits from observations, fragments of legends, and scant remains of early cultures. But little is known of great moments in aboriginal history, successes, failures, discoveries. Hence, there is no record of who really discovered Walker Pass.

Perhaps more pertinent to modern hikers, who must travel on their own resources and endure all hardships that befall them, is the line of self-reliant explorers who have earlier traveled in this territory. We need not suffer what Jedediah Smith suffered, but there is still a considerable amount of that spirit of adventure in anyone who tackles the Pacific Crest Trail, especially as it enters the Sierra Nevada.

Smith, a trapper of New England parentage who pioneered a trail westward from the fledgling United States to Mexican California, may not have encountered the perils and hardships of his predecessors, the early Indians, but even so his trials are difficult to grasp in a modern age of affluence and luxury.

In the 1820s Smith led a band of trappers into California, the first white men from the States to travel those hundreds of miles of hostile wilderness from the East. He was imprisoned for a while by Mexican authorities who suspected him of being a spy. Going on, he and his men became the first to cross the Sierra Nevada (probably at what is now Ebbetts Pass). Later Smith traveled north into Oregon, crossing almost impassable terrain and enduring the perils of Indian massacre. Not long afterward Smith himself was killed on the Santa Fe Trail, probably by Comanche Indians.

Between the time of Jedediah Smith and the Gold Rush, various pioneers went west and crossed or paralleled the present route of the Pacific Crest Trail. Among them were James Ohio Pattie and his father, who were also jailed by the suspicious Mexicans; Ewing Young, trapper and mountain man, with his protégé, Kit Carson; Milton Sublette; George Young; J. J. Warner; David Jackson, of Grand Teton fame, "Old Bill" Williams, and Antoine Robidoux.

After the trappers came the explorers, principally John C. Frémont, who had the audacity to cross the Sierra Nevada in winter (at Carson Pass); he then traveled southward and returned east via Tehachapi Pass.

It is with these adventurers, ramblers, and mountain men that hikers today best identify. Up here are the last vestiges of a wilderness world that the early Indians and explorers knew so well and sometimes had to fight against for survival.

Beyond Walker Pass we climb from desert domains of Joshua tree and sagebrush into the Sierra Nevada, rising in a few miles from

Young owl, Sequoia National Park

4,000 to 8,000 feet. On the way we pass lone piñon pines clinging to steep slopes, or isolated digger pines that suggest a transition zone of vegetation between desert and alpine.

Once again we are at the edge of a precipitous upthrust in the earth's crust. Back at the intersection of the San Gabriel and Tehachapi Mountains, the trail turned sharply from northwest to northeast, from the San Andreas fault to the Garlock fault. Now the trail leaves the Garlock fault, swerves more directly northward, and follows the Sierra fault, one of the most spectacular breaks in the earth's crust. It is also still active, so if the hiker gets troubled by trembling ridges, it should come as no surprise. However, the chances are fairly remote.

Traces of the 1872 earthquake are still visible in small escarpments, offset features, and surface rifts in the Owens Valley. This was one of the powerful earthquakes of historic times, possibly more so than that of 1906 which caused so much damage in San Francisco and vicinity. There was only sparse population in the Owens Valley at the time, and hence fewer than three dozen deaths. Still, the action left long straight scars on the landscape and escarpments at least 20 feet high.

The whole Sierra Nevada is a complex fractured block of the earth's crust torn away, lifted up, and tilted westward. The process of uplift has been so slow—it has taken millions of years to raise the mountains to their present heights—that weathering agents have had plenty of time to do their work.

Even so, the rocks are very hard indeed, and the eastern cliffs and towering peaks have been thrust up faster than erosion could whittle them down, so the high-country hiker sees an abrupt and dramatic change from desert basins to glaciated peaks.

Much of this range is granitic, the so-called Sierra batholith, a deep-seated mass of rock that welled up into the outer earth's crust as much as 200 million years ago. It is flanked by deformed rocks, and even on top of the batholith one may find from place to place a few remnants of rock that once lay above the granite.

The east face of the Sierra Nevada sometimes seems from a distance to be sheer, but it is fairly broken up. The Sierra fault actually amounts to a zone of breakage and slippage along more or less parallel fractures.

We have little time, however, to reflect upon the possibility of the trail giving way under our feet. With chatter and fury, a California woodpecker darts out from the trees and dive-bombs a pair of scrub jays. Before long the trail route has ascended into pine forests, interspersed with meadows and brushy flats, and we are on the Kern Plateau.

This has been called the most glamorous region of the southern Sierra Nevada, perhaps because, owing to relatively late development (the first homesteads were taken in 1918 and roads constructed up the steep sides in 1935), it still retains a great deal of natural charm.

In places there are homes, campgrounds, fences, cattle, and logging trucks, but also lonely grass meadows that contrast with the dry, hot desert below. Fragrant pines fringe the open places and lupines display their colors. Some of the plateau has been considered suitable for designation as wilderness and in time perhaps a considerable segment of it will be reserved for enjoyment of natural values.

The southern edge of the plateau is currently protected in the roadless 62,561-acre Domelands Wilderness, less than 10 miles northwest of Walker Pass. The forest is an open one, and the terrain filled with domelike rocky landmarks, so cross-country hiking is fairly easy there.

Most of the width of the Sierra Nevada lies westward, since the Pacific Crest Trail follows the mountains along their highest, easternmost edge. For hikers with sufficient time to examine side trails, or for weekenders exploring these mountains one section at a time, the southern Sierra Nevada contains several destinations of more than routine interest.

In these uplands are logging and resort towns, campgrounds, roads, trails, abandoned mines and settlements, and an Indian reservation. Modern explorers can also find natural areas to suit their preferences—quiet meadows or thousands of square miles of forest where the singing wind provides a counterpoint to bird and mammal calls. Hawks and eagles fly overhead, and one of the rarest birds, the California condor, comes up to these mountains from its sanctuaries in Los Padres National Forest, more than 100 miles to the southwest.

Hikers in remote areas may encounter deer, bear, and possibly mountain lions. No California grizzlies remain: the last was seen in 1924. Like the Sierra Indians, grizzlies never recovered from the wholesale immigration of marksmen during the Gold Rush of the 1840s.

The hiker who carries a fishing rod can unlimber it on clear streams filled with trout.

The mountains have numerous caves, but their locations are seldom advertised because extensive vandalism has already altered many. There are dozens of groves of giant sequoia in the southern Sierra, the southernmost being Deer Creek Mill grove, about 40 miles northwest of Walker Pass.

Other points of interest include hot springs, old abandoned miners' cabins, waterfalls, springs, and secluded vales with luxuriant vegetation.

The trail climbs higher. We return to regions of whitethorn, which calls for care in negotiating off-route thickets. At some points we pass very near the edge of the steep eastern face of the Sierra

Lodgepole pine cones

Boulders in mountain stream

Nevada, without doubt an impressive drop-off. In one locality the terrain falls from 12,123 to 4,000 feet in less than 4 miles of horizontal distance.

By now the Pacific Crest Trail hiker has become accustomed to the rapid alteration of the surroundings with a rise in elevation. There are also some subtle surprises to be discovered in this wild kingdom.

Down in the Owens Valley, where the weather is less hostile than on the summits but is still harsh enough, the vast shrubby flats consist principally of horsebrush, hopsage and Mormon tea. Above 7,000 feet sagebrush becomes the dominant species.

Jeffrey and lodgepole pines first appear along stream bottoms and then begin to assume command at around 7,500 feet. Farther up, lodgepoles dominate, but sagebrush and bitterbrush exist at nearly 10,000 feet. Even a few representatives of desert flora, such as monkey flower, manage to hang on up to 9,000 feet.

Rising higher, we find the first few scattered whitebark pines, a frequent companion to Pacific Crest Trail hikers. These go on up to tree line, where they sometimes lie sprawled and twisted; though small, they are very old, remarkably capable of surviving in high-altitude environments.

Upper slopes of the Sierra Nevada are often too steep, dry, or soilless to support pine trees, but other plants abound. Along streams or around lakes grow willows, columbines, horsetails, lilies, sedges, and monkshood. On spots where the soil is relatively loose a traveler may pass through patches of quaking aspen.

This may sound somewhat anomalous and gardenlike, and in summer alpine habitats can be positively luxuriant, but there is no mistaking that the vegetation at these elevations leads a rather precarious existence. Although it obviously survives well under natural circumstances, the flora is nevertheless fragile and easily destroyed, and can be disastrously trampled by horses and human beings. This is particularly true in moist meadows near lakes, where paintbrush, monkey flower, fireweed, and rushes try to grow. Such delicateness demands that human visitors walk and camp well back from such areas, admiring them from a distance so that future visitors can also admire them.

More hardy are "outpost" plants on dry and open slopes, at and above tree line. These alpine species include phlox, penstemon, mountain sorrel, and Jacob's ladder.

In wet spots, such as those near snowbanks and along stream courses, grow shooting stars. Wherever pockets of soil manage to collect and provide a little nourishment, the sedges and rushes get established. Out in places of practically no soil and not much moisture, the paintbrush, lupine, and sandwort cling to life.

The hiker who enters these precincts is continuously challenged to figure out how any living organism can survive against so many odds: high winds, low temperatures, short growing seasons, heavy snowfall, summer drought, and intense solar radiation. The answer seems deceptively simple: organisms don't survive if they are not adapted to environmental extremes. The plants we see have succeeded in the face of adversity.

One secret of their success is small size; they hug the ground where the environment is less severe, at least in certain respects. Furthermore, they are perennial; they store food and their daily rate of growth and production is fairly high in this situation. Some plants have seeds that germinate well. Others reproduce vegetatively.

A few species manage to function well in low temperatures, or bear up where the temperature fluctuates widely between day and night. Some flower only when the days become long.

Observing such capabilities, mile after mile along the high trails, we come to realize that we walk not only through patches of colorful mountain flora, but amid some almost miraculous examples of biological evolution. These lie all around, unseen by human travelers who are blinded because they have not yet learned of the immense subtleties before their eyes.

The plants were here long before human beings came, and they gained their exquisite status and occupied their high altitude niches totally as a result of growth and regrowth, success and failure, survival and conquest over thousands or millions of years. Human beings had absolutely nothing to do with their beauty, their adaptations, their evolutionary development (though much to do with their recent protection). We sit back in the greatest of all cathedrals and admire a creative force far older, more competent, and more omnipotent than ours.

Crossing wide meadows and the upper reaches of various tributaries to the Kern River, we make our way past Monache Mountain, Olancha Peak, and finally enter Sequoia National Park at Siberian Pass, elevation 10,920 feet.

Approaching the well-known landmark of Mount Whitney, we are reminded of a major problem on national trails, in national parks, and at wilderness areas across the country and in other parts of the world: too many people attempting to get to the same place at the same time.

Strange that it would be hikers themselves who threaten wild country—hikers who so meticulously care for what they know is rare. But when masses of people concentrate in the same area, without public facilities, there is bound to be a kind of landscape overload, regardless of how each person tries to keep from affecting the environment.

In 1974, taking account of the damage done to the summit of

Mount Whitney

Mount Whitney and the trail up to it, the U.S. Forest Service issued an order restricting travel on that 10.7-mile trail to 75 persons a day.

This may not seem like many people, depending on one's point of view. But during the summer of 1973 at least 15,700 persons had used the trail to Whitney's summit, which averages out to roughly 175 persons a day. It was not unusual, however, for the route to be traveled by as many as 250 persons daily; and during the Labor Day weekend nearly 1,200 climbed the trail.

The summit is rather easy to reach. Hikers drive to Whitney Portal, an Inyo National Forest recreation area 13 miles west of Lone Pine, in the Owens Valley. There at 8,367 feet elevation they park and start up the mountain, entering the John Muir Wilderness. The first night is spent near Mirror Lake or Outpost Camp.

The following day they start at dawn and reach the top by noon. After that, the return to Whitney Portal can be accomplished by sundown.

This relative ease of travel has, in effect, made Whitney's summit a mecca for persons who want to reach the highest point in the "lower 48," and to see something of the spectacular Sierra Nevada at the same time.

There is no question that the view is breathtaking, for the granite walls, snow-spotted slopes, vast deserts, a surrounding group of six peaks over 14,000 feet in elevation, and seemingly endless sky provide the illusory feeling that one is on top of the world and therefore apart from it.

But with so many persons converging on the same area, staying overnight, wandering at random, scattering debris, and depositing bodily wastes where soil is scant or nonexistent, the problems have expanded to crisis proportions. Since part of the trail lies in an officially designated wilderness, and the Wilderness Act of 1964 requires that administering agencies—in this case the U.S. Forest Service—"be responsible for preserving the wilderness character of the area," the large number of people using the trail constituted a violation of the law.

Clearly, human beings can overwhelm a wilderness and modify it as much by hiking in it as by shaking it with sonic booms, laving it with airborne oxidants, or encroaching upon it with summer homes and sprawling recreational developments.

This is especially true at high altitudes, where the vegetation, what little there is, survives under marginal conditions if it survives at all and has not evolved to recover from uncontrolled trampling.

Thus the Forest Service was compelled to issue its order restricting public use of Mount Whitney. However unpalatable that may be, it is inevitable, and is not the fault of the Forest Service;

rather, it can be attributed to other factors, at the origin of which seems to be excessive human fecundity.

Hence we have almost a landmark in human history, a public agency compelled to do in the national forests what people themselves may have to do on the total surface of this finite planet—limit the number of persons who enter.

Throughout the United States, permits have become a requirement for overnight stays in most if not all wilderness areas. This provides a convenient means of controlling not only numbers of visitors but, through required informational programs, behavior as well. Ten times as many people might be admitted to a wilderness and all enjoy it, if their behavior is restrained, than would be the case of uncontrolled visitation and random use. This concept has been tested by experience and inserted into planning and management efforts—such as the permit system, new regulations regarding livestock, instructions on where to camp, and limits to the use of firewood.

Prospective hikers on the Pacific Crest Trail can avoid heavily used routes by adroit planning. There are sufficient forest folders, guidebooks, maps, and current information to permit one to select less crowded trails. There are also wilderness permits, lists of applicable regulations, and maps of side trails to be taken.

Hikers should also plan to carry their own fuel, use drably colored packs and tents, avoid the use of motorized vehicles, keep dogs at home, limit the size of party, carry out all trash, travel with someone rather than alone, rely on their own legs instead of on horses, collect no firewood (especially in alpine areas), and perhaps in places where there is high fire danger, stay out of the wilderness altogether. However undesirable these restrictions appear to be, it is still an inescapable truism that innumerable people cannot enjoy a wilderness together.

In a sense, the Pacific Crest Trail is a path through a museum, and in museums one does not crawl over the specimens or camp in exhibit cases. Until the number of human beings declines a bit, the behavior of visitors to wilderness areas may have to become more like that of museumgoers who are allowed to look but seldom to touch.

There is only one Sierra Nevada.

Snow plant

5

John Muir Trail

Up we climb with glad exhilaration.

John Muir, *The Yosemite*, 1912

WE ARE NOW in the high country, and going higher.

Between Mount Whitney and the Devils Postpile the Pacific Crest Trail achieves its highest elevations. And this is one of the most up-and-down parts of the entire route. Time after time the trail rises above tree line to 10,000 or 11,000 feet, only to cross a pass or ridge and descend on the other side to a meadow, creek, or canyon at 8,000 or 9,000 feet and then repeat the process.

This gigantic roller-coaster experience consists of exhausting climbs and bone-jarring descents over steep switchbacks. The going can be cruel, the uphill seemingly endless. Creeks must be jumped, waded, or—mercifully—crossed on logs. The trail may be strewn with rocks or even consist of steps cut in cliffs.

Eventually we reach the highest elevation on the Pacific Crest Trail, 13,200 feet, at Forester Pass, on the boundary between Sequoia and Kings Canyon National Parks.

The weather at the passes can be windy and cold, but the hiker perspires. At these elevations the heart thumps, the lungs burn, the eyes squint in the brightness, the skin turns red from intense solar radiation.

Hikers may suffer serious sickness due to excess exertion and the deficiency of oxygen at high altitude. Obviously persons susceptible to such problems, or those with weakened hearts, should not even attempt to hike in these realms except with the consent of a doctor.

For miles the trail, in its rising and falling, passes towering peaks, innumerable lakes, plunging waterfalls, and turbulent waters in narrow chutes. The hiker's mind absorbs a thousand sights that blend into a montage of polished granite walls, sheltered vales, grassy meadows, alpine flower gardens, lodgepole pine forests, stunted whitebark pines at the upper frontiers of growth, dramatic gorges, avalanche chutes. . . .

Then there are sounds, aromas, happenings—

It is almost too much. Travelers beset with constant curiosity too often want to stop and spend more time at a particular spot. Philosophers want to contemplate the scenery. Photographers want to wait a few more minutes until the clouds and shadows are positioned just right.

The question then is how to reach the night's destination.

It may be better to have no destination at all, no schedule, no itinerary. But if food runs out, the modern hiker in all probability would be hard put to survive, as John Muir did, with a bag of tea and sugar.

The trail leads into treeless, glacier-scoured basins whose slopes and walls and peaks engulf the traveler, almost diminishing the tiny human being to insignificance. One doesn't mind; it is refreshing to be where people are not trying to dominate the environment.

However, the hiker does pass numerous places where the effects of human use appear. Overused campsites abound, especially along stream banks, lakeshores, and at picturesque spots where the alpine terrain has simply been worn out by the trample of thousands of human bodies. Except for an occasional hut, there are no amenities. People have been on their own, which is to say that they have had to use the resources at hand. And the resources, at least in certain places, have been too fragile to withstand the onslaught.

Alpine meadows have relatively soft soil, partly covered with thin mats of delicate vegetation. A footpath trod by many boots is washed out during storms and times of snowmelt, and it becomes a trench. Humans and horses then avoid the trench (often dusty) and follow a parallel route on soft matted vegetation. The process is repeated and eventually half a dozen parallel trenches are dug. What is the end of it? A dozen trenches? Two dozen?

Worse yet, a hiker setting off on side excursions across a meadow leaves faint impressions in the soil. Another hiker, curious, follows. And another. Paths are soon clearly indicated and ultimately worn into the meadow like a network of random grooves. The place becomes as crisscrossed with trails as a Texas cattle ranch.

No hiker intended this to happen. But the destruction, defacing, marring is done. It is real. It gets worse. In the end the problem falls on park and forest administrators to analyze what is happening, establish some sort of guide to the "carrying capacity" of fragile

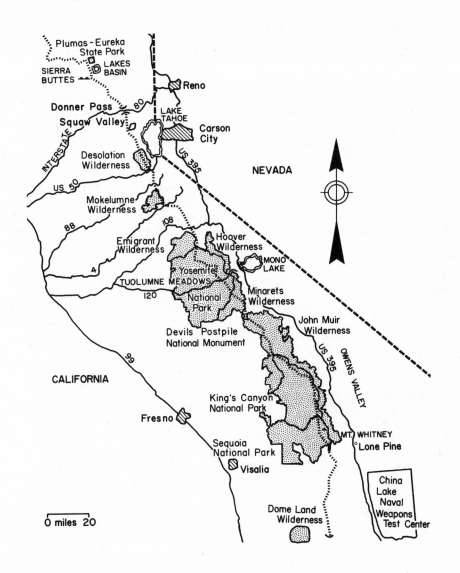

THE PACIFIC CREST TRAIL IN THE SIERRA NEVADA

areas, and put into effect the rules and restrictions required to prevent destructive overuse. The Swiss model may some day prevail: in the Swiss National Park, near Zernez, no one strays off the trail or stays overnight in the wild.

Hitchcock Lakes, Wallace Creek, Mount Williamson, Baxter Pass, Big Pete Meadows, Goddard Divide—the Pacific Crest Trail seems to pass a gauntlet of natural features named in honor of human beings. Some names given to features in this region are descriptive and appropriate: Split Mountain, Vermilion Cliffs, Bear Ridge, Fish Creek, and Pumice Butte.

Others are more mysterious: Muah Mountain, Taboose Pass, Dumbbell Lakes, Disappointment Peak, Jackass Dike, and Hell for Sure Lake. A few recall the Indian era, such as Piute Pass, Chagoopa Plateau, Mount Kaweah, and Tuolumne Meadows.

Perhaps it would be more appropriate if nothing here had been named after human beings at all, or even by them. If wilderness objects must be named to satisfy human vanity, better such designations as the Citadel, Granite Stairway, and Cathedral Range. Or perhaps a return to Indian names that graphically describe the natural objects.

Happily, we are not obliged to accept tradition and can rename anything we see. Up here the traveler can be a private Board of Geographic Names. If any person should be allotted a peak, it might be John Muir, who appreciated the mountains so thoroughly, discovered and described their glacial features in the face of ridicule by scientists, fought to save the most beautiful parts of them, and left written records of the original beauty of the range.

The John Muir Trail, between Mount Whitney and Tuolumne Meadows, has now become part of the Pacific Crest Trail. Along this section of more than 200 miles are some of the most spectacular parts of the Sierra Nevada. The hiker gains sweeping views from passes and peaks in the eastern parts of Sequoia and Kings Canyon National Parks. The trail crosses numerous tributaries of the Kern River and passes close to the eastern edge of that extraordinarily straight, glacier-scoured phenomenon, Kern Canyon.

Going northward, the trail winds in and out among alpine forests, glacial basins, and lakes on the upper reaches of the Kings River.

Turning northwestward, it enters the John Muir Wilderness, part of Sierra National Forest, then passes through Inyo National Forest, Devils Postpile National Monument and the Minarets Wilderness before entering Yosemite National Park at Donohue Pass.

This highest section of the Pacific Crest Trail is a raw land where wind and snow predominate most of the year. Ice freezes in the cracks and splits off fragments of granite the size of slivers or houses. The result is a jumbled terrain fairly difficult to negotiate because it is broken and angular, and the fragments are precariously perched, sometimes giving way under one's feet.

Falling rock is one of the major hazards to be faced when one is scaling peaks in the Sierra Nevada. Professional climbers are especially fearful of rock slabs dislodged by climbers just above them. Where smooth and polished or where lightly covered with a few sand grains, the rocks are also slippery. Anyone who falls up here discovers that granite is one of the hardest of rocks and that this locality is very far from medical aid.

No such problems affect the vegetation. Huge pines exist in some of the most precarious places, dwarfed by the cliffs that support them. Vertical crevices, where it seems no soil could possibly have accumulated, may support shrubs, banks of ferns, and clusters of flowers. Hardy black lichens grow on exposed rock surfaces.

Sometimes we make our way through odd terrain where boulders are so scattered across the landscape that it looks as though some giant had broken off a mountain peak and hurled fragments of it in all directions. These glacial erratics lie where melting ice abandoned them: perched on barren rock or partially buried in meadows.

We are surrounded by the residue and evidence of glaciers, and it is hard to realize, on days when the sun bakes the high country, that this domain was once locked in ice. A few patches of ice and snow remain, but only remnants of what was.

The Sierra Nevada is believed to have been engulfed by glacial ice moving out from local ice caps, spreading over the mountains in three or four stages. In some places the ice reached depths of 2,000 to 3,000 feet as the glaciers slowly but relentlessly flowed downslope along existing stream valleys. During times of maximum ice thickness only the highest peaks and domes stood out as islands in a sea of ice.

We can readily conjecture what went on in those days, knowing the present-day habits of glaciers. The smoothed slopes and scoured canyons we see now, for example, are almost surely the results of ice impact and friction. Erosional forces generated by such weights of ice, such relentless energy, and such irresistible motion are hard to conceive, but the planing of rock as hard as this could only have been done by immense moving masses of ice over centuries or millenniums.

Now the glaciers are gone, but ice is still at work. When water seeps into crevices or under the loosened "onion skin" layers of granite on rounded domes, it occasionally freezes and expands to disrupt another layer or another ledge.

In addition to cracked ledges, spalling domes, and sun-bright mirror surfaces of polished granite, we see in the high country numerous small basins (cirques) that were scooped out by glaciers. These have become filled with water and some of the resulting cirque lakes are slowly being filled with sediment and organic debris. In time they should become meadows.

All the lakes, ice, and glaciers, as well as the continuous erosion of these mountains, are due in large measure to the snow or rain that fall or the water that collects from fog. For that reason the incoming clouds, including the building up of great thunderheads in summer, have almost a supreme significance, even apart from the supplying of water to sustain life.

Though summer days in the Sierra Nevada are seldom rainy, there are often dramatic clouds, appearing perhaps as tufts over the high peaks about midmorning, then ballooning, rolling, and seething. This performance may go on all day, at different atmospheric levels, the exploding white mushrooms contrasting vividly with dark blue sky. Such threatening postures seem to presage a dire deluge, but the clouds do not deliver, except on rare and unusual occasions. Winter is ordinarily the time of rain and flood.

Coincident with this natural evolution of clouds are jet trails that cross the sky, drift, expand, coalesce, and then dissolve into a haze that diminishes the brightness and sparkle that might have been below. This is anathema to photographers, and how long it can go on without altering the natural growth rhythms of wild vegetation is difficult to say.

Absorbed with the clouds, the difficulties of traversing the terrain, and the drama of alpine country, a newcomer unaccustomed to the altitude may proceed too rapidly, oblivious to the rarefied air, and begin to experience headaches. But with gradual adaptation to the environment these should disappear.

The hiker may also become accustomed to the sharp cold, biting wind, burning sun, flying dust, or threats of storm and lightning.

But the surroundings do not always threaten; we are overwhelmed, from place to place, by forms, shapes, and colors. For example, no red is more vivid than that of paintbrush petals emerging from morning shadows and illuminated from behind by the rays of a rising sun.

The red mountain heather (a heath rather than a true heather) forms showy mats at high elevations, its stamens projecting like armed bristles from the rose-purple corollas. White heather has nodding flowers with red caps, like clusters of fragile bells that might ring in the mountain breeze.

In due course, the traveler will become familiar with an extraordinary variety of wildflowers, for the route passes through some of the richest botanical displays in North America. These crowd upon the trail from both sides, in frequently dense patches from here to Canada. With a natural curiosity, the Pacific Crest Trail hiker will become something of a botanist.

In alpine and subalpine zones of the Sierra Nevada is an elegant alpine lily that grows in protected places; unlike some of its relatives which have pendant blossoms, its yellow and orange blossoms spotted with maroon open upward to the sun. The tubular blue flowers of gentian may be seen blooming up to 10,000 feet. Sulphur flower, a member of the buckwheat family, combines with paintbrush to turn dry open ridges and sunny slopes into a mass of scarlet and yellow.

Occasionally one comes to a tiny cul-de-sac sheltered from severe mountain weather, a place overhung by a ledge and supplied with water from seepage. This is an ideal spot for ferns and moss, and is also the milieu for bright yellow *Mimulus*, or monkey flower, so-called because the arrangement of its petals resembles a monkey's face.

In similar spots grow red columbines, a ruby-red sprinkle of color when illuminated by the sun in otherwise shady places. The long red petal spurs and yellow stamens shine like beacons, and before long hummingbirds respond.

Sometimes exceptional grace and beauty may be discovered in rather small flowers, as in the elephant head or stonecrop. By leaning close we get a better appreciation of the stonecrop's delicate red and yellow flowers and leaves so tightly packed and succulent that they seem about to burst.

But few plants of high granite crevices are as striking as penstemon, a member of the snapdragon family. Its small magenta trumpets cluster in warm clefts of black and white rock, producing one of the most dazzling of Sierra wildflower displays.

One moment the hiker is on an open, breezy pass amid barren patches of rock, the next in a soft vale of ferns. About three dozen species of ferns grow in the Sierra Nevada, some widespread but so small and hidden that they are frequently overlooked, such as the little grape fern.

The fragile maidenhair fern overhangs moist places up to 10,000 feet elevation. The golden polypody hangs in lacy curtains from crevices where water seeps. Other types grow to fair dimensions, such as bracken and lady ferns, up to 4 feet high, and the chain fern, up to 8 feet.

Were it not for all the water in the high country, vegetation would be less widespread. And water is most reliable in the ubiquitous lakes.

"Among the many unlooked-for-treasures that are bound up and hidden away in the depths of Sierra solitudes," said John Muir, "none more surely charm and surprise all kinds of travelers than the glacier lakes."

He estimated that there were altogether 1,500 lakes in the Sierra

Nevada, not counting innumerable pools, ponds, and tarns. Nearly all are in the alpine and subalpine regions, many nestled in bowl-shaped cirques. Where soil has collected, a little greenery grows, including wildflowers, willows, and small patches of stunted pines.

Waters from these high-perched lakes slide or catapult down the slope into a canyon or valley below. Some lakes lie in a chain of bowllike rocky basins connected by streamlets of rippling cascades. If low and well protected, the lakes may take on something of the character of paradise—surrounded by deep pine forests, decorated with aspen groves, lined with masses of purple lupine.

Between lakes, we become intimately acquainted with streams, which accompany us down canyons, cross our path, bathe us in spray and fill the air with roaring thunder or delicate music. After a while this constant symphony grows on us, and when away from it we may not be fully content until, through a pine grove, we hear the rippling obbligatos again.

The waters are pure and good to drink except where they have been contaminated from overuse by people and horses. The pools are like liquid lenses, magnifying the sands that glitter with flakes of gold, and observers may have one of those pangs of excitement that brought hordes of prospectors into this range during Gold Rush days. Anybody may search for nuggets—and perhaps even find one.

But it is not very likely that the modern prospector will find any of nature's treasure vaults that have not already been probed several times in the past century.

For those able to appreciate it, a more abundant treasure lies in the liquid art of the river pools. As seen through swirling currents, the rocks assume abstract patterns that are never the same two seconds in a row. Transient in shape and color, like flames of a campfire, they dissolve into other forms before we can begin to assess their designs. Such fleeting visions can be captured only through photography or in the traveler's mind.

Occasionally the waters shoot the chutes—smooth granite troughs fashioned by glaciers. Or fan out over aprons and run hissing downslope at high speed. Cracks in the rock may interrupt this flow, adding geometric designs to the apron and making the waters glance off sideways, creating foamy surflike patterns.

When these streams fall at a greater angle, their waters tumble with white violence from ledge to ledge, splitting and rejoining, spilling over fallen logs or sliding under them, and splashing the adjacent rocks and moss with spray. In cases of extreme turbulence, such as during the height of spring runoff, the seething, plunging waters are totally white and the stream turns into a violent maelstrom with a deafening roar.

Where less violent, the waters are full of organisms: trout, hellgrammites, larvae, worms, nymphs, crayfish, striders on the sur-

face, beetles diving, ouzels at the water's edge or sometimes under-
neath the surface. Kingfishers, sandpipers, beavers, raccoons, water
shrews, and other species come to drink or search for aquatic food.

The interactions of all these, with each other and with the
system in which they evolved, are extremely complex and little
known. Streamside observations of ecological mechanisms could keep
us occupied from sunup to dark, and then some.

And the same is true for meadows, which are nearly always
lively places. A streamlet cascades between willow-lined banks,
singing over stones. Young pines march in disoriented patterns, as
though disarrayed from being compressed so many months under
deep snow.

Specks of white glow ghostlike through the trees—the granite
boulders left haphazardly by melting glaciers. Infinite arrangements
of these can occupy a hiker's time, disrupting any schedule he may
have been foolish enough to try to keep. They are strewn in unexpected places and unexpected patterns. Some are rounded, some
cleft and slabbed as though by frost, some lined with veins of quartz,
some covered with glittering feldspar crystals.

In many cases the grassy mat at our feet may be little more
than an inch thick, for not much soil has formed since the melting
of the glaciers. In other places the ice left thick deposits of sand
and debris, and rich soil has filled up alpine lakes. "The sod is close
and fine," wrote John Muir, "and so complete that you cannot see
the ground; and at the same time so brightly enameled with flowers
and butterflies that it may well be called a garden-meadow. . . ."

Each spring the grass in richer meadows turns a dark green, and
then, with the burgeoning and flowering of shooting stars, a wash
of purple transforms the vales. Like domestic cyclamens, which are
also in the primrose family, shooting stars hang at the tips of leafless
stalks, remindful of exploding rockets bursting into a shower of
color. The close-pressed stamens form a protruding dark cone that
seems to lead the magenta-colored petals back to earth. Shooting
stars not only cover meadows, but grow in small clusters in isolated
open spots. Few flowers better express the gentle grandeur of the
Sierra Nevada.

Suddenly a loud piercing shriek stops us in our tracks. It fills
the air, echoing from a nearby cliff and reverberating from wall to
wall in the high cirque.

The echoes fade slowly, bouncing from dome to dome, for
at this high elevation no forests exist to absorb the sound.

Then there is silence. Nothing moves. We wonder if we really
heard anything at all, whether it was a dream, or merely some trick
of the inner ear.

It comes again. Now, at least, we find out where it's coming from. We scan the naked rocks, the ledges, shrubs, patches of meadow. . . .

Nothing. No movement. No shrieking witch. No darting eagle. No human voice. Only silence again. We wonder if the altitude has begun to produce in us some dizzying effect that leads to hallucinations.

Again it comes. Louder than ever, filling the vale with multiple echoes. And then we see a patch of brown and yellow fur, perhaps a foot tall, sitting on a rock, so unmoving as to be nearly indistinguishable from the surroundings.

The animal seems almost regal, with every appearance of owning all the terrain it sees. To be sure, the broken, slabbing granite peaks dwarf it; white snow patches gleam more brightly than its yellow fur. But the marmot cares not. Its golden shoulders and yellow back are only to be envied by nearby residents. It is a master of its domain.

Sitting on its haunches, it looks every bit the rodent it is, although more paunchy than others of its clan. The black ring around its nose gives the impression that a muzzle has been strapped into place.

And then we have a pang of pity. That coat—so full and shaggy and warm; how any animal so covered with fur can survive the intense solar radiation at this altitude is incomprehensible. By all odds, the creature should be roasting in the midday sun. Does it roll in the snow to cool off? Or retreat to the shade?

It defies us by flattening out on a rock and basking in the sunlight.

The alpine uplands, far from being barren, harbor a considerable fauna, and the hiker on Sierra trails soon comes to know them. The marmot's closer relatives—beavers, ground squirrels, chipmunks—thrive in high places. Sometimes a small meadow will be so full of ground squirrels running from hole to hole that it looks as though someone had unleashed a collection of oversize Mexican jumping beans.

The key to their location is, of course, the availability of food. Seeds and vegetation are staple; the nuts of whitebark pine, for example, are consumed by Clark's nutcrackers and alpine chipmunks, the latter having been observed at elevations above 13,000 feet. Shrews must live where they can find and consume insects. Coyotes and weasels must be able to find such morsels as mice, gophers, and wood rats.

Among the most common mammals in the Sierra Nevada are deer, which move down from the high country in winter. As for other large mammals in the upper parts of the range, mountain lions and bighorns occur but in such limited numbers that visitors seldom see them. In fact, the eyes of human beings are generally not con-

Sierra Nevada, Yosemite National Park

ditioned to detect wildlife along the trail. Most people see wild animals by accident, being untrained to recognize tracks, meadow trails, scats, and other evidence. Unless hikers slow down and observe carefully, they may see little life at all, barring a confrontation with black bears.

Of course, they may be lucky to hear mammals such as the marmot. Pikas also put on a vocal performance, intended to alert the neighborhood that an intruder is nearby. Pikas, related to hares and rabbits, inhabit bouldery slopes where it is hard to see gray fur against gray rock. Talus jumbles contain abundant passageways for warmth and protection, and even in winter the pika, well adapted to high country, survives by feeding on dried vegetation stored up the previous summer.

Another place to look for life is in high-elevation streams, where such residents as yellow-legged frogs may be found. We may well wonder how amphibians live in a land that is frozen so much of the year. The secret is that these frogs, lacking time to mature during a single short summer, remain in the larval stage over winter, probably in water under ice; thus they take two summers to come to full growth.

A traveler is likely to notice birds more often than mammals throughout the Pacific Crest Trail. They fly around crags and across meadows or along streams, some producing screeches that make them hard to miss. We see gulls on lakes and hear killdeers in wet places. Where streams have fish, there is the unmistakable rattle of kingfishers. We note that flickers and Arctic three-toed and hairy woodpeckers inhabit wooded areas. So do Steller's jays, whose loud chatter can be heard long distances through the woods.

If the mating season is not over, we may hear songs of meadowlark and hermit thrush. Mourning doves and horned owls occasionally venture up from the lowlands. By contrast, Oregon juncos live up here year round and occasionally descend to lower regions.

Hikers in the Sierra Nevada are likely to become best acquainted with Clark's nutcrackers, but white-crowned sparrows are also abundant, especially in grassy and shrubby places. Less well known is a bird of the highest elevations, the Sierra Nevada rosy finch, which feeds on insects frozen in the snow and flying in the cold air; it also eats seeds, and so can survive when insects are not available.

Smaller transients may be difficult to see, such as rufous hummingbirds that pass through the high country on southbound migratory flights in July and August.

Of all birds in the Sierra Nevada, the most unusual may well be water ouzels. Few terrestrial birds make water so much a part of their lives. Ouzels are born near it in a nest made of spray-washed moss; they live near it, dive into it, and even walk along the bottom of pools.

The ouzel is not a water bird, however, and has no webs between its toes. Nevertheless, its dense covering of feathers helps to shed water and retain warmth. It is the size of a robin, and when perched on a log or rock at the water's edge characteristically bobs up and down, which gives it the name "dipper."

Its music is a bell-like note, tuneful like the falling water around it, and John Muir avowed that no mountain bird cheered him so much in his wanderings through the high country. "No need of spring sunshine to thaw *his* song, "Muir wrote, "for it never freezes."

Muir devotes a chapter to this bird in his book *The Mountains of California*. He also has much to say about "the wildest animal I ever saw,—a fiery, sputtering little bolt of life," the Douglas squirrel, now called the chickaree.

Muir's toleration of all things wild and his fascination with nature were phenomenal. Even the coldest rocks were alive to him in one way or another. "How softly these rocks are adorned," he wrote, "and how fine and reassuring the company they keep."

In the forty-five years he roamed in the Sierra Nevada, between 1868 and 1914, he examined the length of the range as no other human beings had or have. Modern men call their sojourns hikes. Muir called them capital excursions.

Some were almost lethal excursions for Muir. He usually went alone, without any thought of safety or rescue, and disregarded dangers as though he were some daredevil. He got caught in an avalanche and rode it safely to the bottom of the slope. He was hit by falling ice, nearly fell over the brink of Yosemite Falls, was tossed by gale winds in a treetop and shaken by severe earthquakes. But he was merely out where the action was, regardless of danger, and believed that "these mountain mansions are decent, delightful, even divine, places to die in, compared with the doleful chambers of civilization."

It is perhaps this intense interest in the surrounding world that the Pacific Crest Trail hiker will have in common with Muir. To our minds, one of the adventures that best suggests his attitude and temperament was his reaction to an earthquake in Yosemite Valley.

This series of tremors began March 26, 1872, and caused considerable damage and death in Owens Valley on the eastern side of the Sierra Nevada, as has already been recounted. Muir described it thus:

At half-past two o'clock of a moonlit morning in March, I was awakened by a tremendous earthquake, and though I had never before enjoyed a storm of this sort, the strange thrilling motion could not be mistaken, and I ran out of my cabin, both glad and frightened, shouting, "A noble earthquake! A noble earthquake!" feeling sure I was going to learn something. The shocks were so violent and varied, and succeeded one another so closely, that I had to balance myself carefully in walking as if on the deck of a ship among waves, and it seemed impossible that the high cliffs of the Valley could escape being shattered. In particular, I feared that the sheer-fronted Sentinel Rock, towering above my cabin, would be shaken down, and I took shelter back of a large yellow pine, hoping that it might protect me from at least the smaller outbounding boulders. For a minute or two the shocks became more and more violent—flashing horizontal thrusts mixed with a few twists and battering, explosive, upheaving jolts,—as if Nature were wrecking her Yosemite temple, and getting ready to build a still better one.

I was now convinced before a single boulder had fallen that earthquakes were the talus-makers and positive proof soon came. It was a calm moonlight night, and no sound was heard for the first minute or so, save low, muffled, underground, bubbling rumblings, and the whispering and rustling of the agitated trees, as if Nature were holding her breath. Then, suddenly, out of the strange silence and strange motion there came a tremendous roar. The Eagle Rock on the south wall, about a half a mile up the Valley, gave way and I saw it falling in thousands of the great boulders I had so long been studying, pouring to the Valley floor in a free curve luminous from friction, making a terribly sublime spectacle—an arc of glowing, passionate fire, fifteen hundred feet span, as true in form and as serene in beauty as a rainbow in the midst of the stupendous, roaring rock-storm. The sound was so tremendously deep and broad and earnest, the whole earth like a living creature seemed to have at last found a voice and to be calling to her sister planets. In trying to tell something of the size of this awful sound it seems to me that if all the thunder of all the storms I had ever heard were condensed into one roar it would not equal this rock-roar at the birth of a mountain talus. . . .

The first severe shocks were soon over, and eager to examine the new-born talus I ran up the Valley in the moonlight and climbed upon it before the huge blocks, after their fiery flight, had come to complete rest. They were slowly settling into their places, chafing, grating against one another, groaning, and whispering; but no motion was visible except in a stream of small fragments pattering down the face of the cliff. A cloud of dust particles, lighted by the moon, floated out across the whole breadth of the Valley, forming a ceiling that lasted until after sunrise, and the air was filled with the odor of crushed Douglas spruces from a grove that had been mowed down and mashed like weeds. . . .

During the third severe shock the trees were so violently shaken that the birds flew out with frightened cries. In particular, I noticed two robins flying in terror from a leafless oak, the branches of which swished and quivered as if struck by a heavy battering-ram. . . .

It was long before the Valley found perfect rest. The rocks trembled more or less every day for over two months, and I kept a bucket of water on my table to learn what I could of the movements. The blunt thunder in the depths of the mountains was usually followed by sudden jarring, horizontal thrusts from the northward, often succeeded by twisting, up-jolting movements. . . .

All Nature's wildness tells the same story—the shocks and outbursts of earthquakes, volcanoes, geysers, roaring, thundering waves and floods, the silent uprush of sap in plants, storms of every sort—each and all are the orderly beauty-making love-beats of Nature's heart.

The word Muir used most often to describe his own response to nature's actions was "rejoicing." He never worried about getting caught out, stranded, or marooned, even in the deep snow of winter. He simply spent the night "without suffering anything worth minding."

He was perhaps history's leading apostle of doing what you wanted when you wanted, and thus unencumbered himself of the so-called necessities of life. He could take off at any hour of the day or night, in any weather, any temperature, and with little more than sugar, tea, and flour in his pack. Moreover, he stretched his long legs as few others could and covered more ground in shorter time than would ordinarily be recommended. But when he stopped, it was sometimes to observe what most people would regard as the merest thing; and he stopped for a long time to observe and study until he was thoroughly satisfied. That is the stuff wild freedom is made of.

The landscape, to him, "stretched sublimely away in fresh wildness—a manuscript written by the hand of Nature alone."

But Muir wrote his own manuscripts and published them, and was in time visited by such eminent persons as John Burroughs, Ralph Waldo Emerson, and President Theodore Roosevelt.

He became so incensed at the immense hordes of starving cattle and sheep that trampled the wild subalpine gardens and meadows in the vicinity of the passes that he was naturally led into a career of conservation. Without a doubt, he widely stimulated the protection of natural areas in the Sierra Nevada.

We recall his crusades and his life in these mountains as we hike among the boulders and flowers he revered. To him the Sierra Nevada was in many ways a "Range of Light."

Yet it has also been a "Range of Darkness," for in these tragic hills the exalted role of humans conserving nature has been counterbalanced by the killing of Indians and wildlife. With the great nineteenth-century influx of prospectors, miners, farmers, and other settlers during the Gold Rush, the hitherto remote and peaceful sanctum of native Indians was invaded. The newcomers shot both Indians and grizzly bears for similar reasons: competition for the same habitat, fear, anger, sport. According to one estimate, nearly 50,000 Indians were killed in the twenty years following the discovery of gold. By 1910 the Indian population of the region had been reduced by nearly 90 percent.

There were five general groups of Indians in these mountains, the Yokuts, Miwok, Maidu, Washo, and Mono. The higher up they lived, the poorer they were, yet they moved about and traded and so were not entirely poverty-stricken. They exchanged pine nuts, basket-making materials, obsidian, clay, paint, and other items. They lived in various kinds of shelters, including caves whose roofs are still blackened with the smoke of centuries.

After the general orgy of killing—so one-sided because Sierra Indians were much less warlike than their counterparts to the east—the human inhabitants of the range had changed from brown to white.

These thoughts sober us as we hike through a land our ancestors took by force and afterwards tore up with roads and laved with toxic air pollutants. Of course, the biological nature of animal life is survival of the fittest, and so whether we like it or not, this progression of events followed natural laws. But man ought to have a destiny other than murder and subsequent environmental rapacity, and happily is developing laws other than those that predestine the lower animals.

We drop down out of the highest elevations briefly and reach the Devils Postpile. This is not a stack of wooden posts and has nothing to do with the devil, but it is one of the world's best exposures of columnar basalt.

This lava was forced out of the earth through a fissure that opened in Mammoth Pass more than 915,000 years ago. The molten material poured out into the middle fork of the San Joaquin River and filled the valley from side to side. This smoking pool contracted as it cooled and cracked into nearly uniform polygonal patterns.

The "posts" today average two feet in diameter. Some reach 60 feet in height, and have four to seven sides. Above a pile of broken columns that looks like rubble beneath the Jordanian Temple of Artemis at Jerash, they present a dramatic facade.

Glaciers and other forces of erosion have scooped out or worn

Devils Postpile National Monument

Glacier-polished surface, Devils Postpile

away most of the columns originally formed. Ice also smoothed off the top of the columns so that we have a polished basalt "pavement" resembling a cross section of a giant congealed honeycomb.

Eventually all the posts will fall, for water seeps into the cracks, freezes, expands, and exerts a force not even solid rock can resist.

The area was made a national monument in 1911 and is administered by the Superintendent of Yosemite National Park. Within the boundaries the middle fork of the San Joaquin River plunges over a lava precipice and falls 140 feet in a roaring, dramatic cascade called Rainbow Falls. The Pacific Crest Trail goes within a mile of it.

Not far off the route are obsidian lava flows containing great chunks of black volcanic glass. Flow patterns of the original lava outpourings are revealed in glistening surfaces, a bonanza for artists seeking unusual design and patterns in nature.

Northwest from the Devils Postpile, the Pacific Crest Trail proceeds into the Minarets Wilderness, passes under Two Teats Mountain and comes to jewellike lakes below the Ritter Range. Reflected in these lakes are spires of the Minarets, a row of sharply eroded peaks that bear resemblance to Near Eastern prayer towers.

The lower regions are covered with open coniferous forests interrupted by rounded granitic domes. The domes and barren basins become more prominent higher up, and eventually the forest fades away. On higher peaks, where shade prevails, patches of snow and ice remain throughout the summer.

At Donohue Pass we enter Yosemite National Park. Spread out to the west for 761,320 acres, the park conserves what is to us the greatest concentration of natural wonders along the Pacific Crest Trail. Its major features—Half Dome, Clouds Rest, El Capitan, groves of sequoia trees—are so well known that little need be said of them here. Likewise, some of the numerous waterfalls in the park are world-renowned, several being more than 1,000 feet high. Master of all, Yosemite Falls measures 2,425 feet from brink to base, second only to Venezuela's Angel Falls for the world record.

Yosemite was one of the world's first landmarks in the conservation of natural areas, the valley portion of it having been set aside by President Abraham Lincoln in 1864. It is interesting to observe that even in the days of mining and Indian killing, articulate explorers enjoyed the mountains for their natural beauty rather than for their gold and sought solitude in them more than routes for railroads or pastures for sheep.

Accounts of their ascents of difficult peaks and domes make interesting reading, especially as they were done in an era lacking the modern accoutrements that make mountaineering safer and easier.

We have already mentioned John Muir, but it would be in-

Yosemite Valley in winter

appropriate to disregard Clarence King, a young geologist who, when just over thirty years old, wrote a series of sketches from his journals and in 1872 published them in book form: *Mountaineering in the Sierra Nevada.*

King had been on the field surveying staff of Professor J. D. Whitney, State Geologist of California, and afterwards headed the Fortieth Parallel Survey, which examined a swath of wild America between the Rocky Mountains and the Sierra Nevada.

His adventures among these peaks are dramatic fare, strengthened by what was then known of the regional geologic structure. He disagreed with John Muir in the running battle of whether glaciers had a major role in shaping the Sierra Nevada (and in this he lost to Muir). But he also had a sharp appreciation of sunsets, pure air, and breathtaking views. The summits, he said, were "forever new, full of individuality, rich in detail, and coloring themselves anew under every cloud change or hue of heaven, they lay you under their spell."

Two of his chapters are devoted to the ascent and descent of a peak he named Mount Tyndall. His words on reaching the summit would be well comprehended by high-country hikers:

"At last, when almost at the top, we paused to take breath, and then all walked out upon the crest, laid off our packs, and sat down together upon the summit of the ridge, and for a few moments not a word was spoken."

At Tuolumne Meadows the Pacific Crest Trail comes to a highway, the first since Walker Pass, some 200 miles to the south. It is only a brief intrusion, for the trail soon leaves the road behind, and the hiker begins a section once called the Tahoe-Yosemite Trail.

The upland meadows here are good places to start out on side trips, which are possible in all parts of the Sierra Nevada. In the Yosemite region one can obtain detailed information, including current regulations regarding back-country use. The adjacent national forests also possess complex systems of hiking trails.

From the summit of Mount Dana (13,053 feet) one has an extraordinary view of all of Mono Lake far below, that saline body of water that is a remnant of the vast ancient system of desert lakes.

Worthwhile hikes lead to Gaylor Lakes, the historic Golden Crown mines, Clouds Rest, and other destinations. Many of these are strenuous all-day excursions from Tuolumne Meadows. These trips may be taken at any time of the year, although access may be more difficult when roads are closed by snow.

Actually, summer is the least desirable time to be in the Sierra Nevada. It is pleasant enough, but there are simply more interesting things going on during the other three seasons.

The Pacific Crest Trail hiker, in the course of so many abrupt changes in elevation, may encounter two or three seasons on a single trip. If flowers are blooming in the lower valleys, there may be remnants of winter on higher slopes. Or when the first winter snows fall on the summits, say in October, autumn is still in full swing below.

Autumn here is not as spectacular as in the Rocky Mountains because sweeping groves of golden aspen are less extensive. Still, patches of them can be stunningly beautiful, especially when back-lighted by the morning or evening sun.

However, it would be a poor autumn that depended solely on aspen for color. The cinnamon hues of dogwood leaves, together with deep blue sky, form an unusually complementary color scheme. Much the same can be said for oaks, whose leaves illumine the meadows in autumn or float like golden rafts down the dwindling rivers.

The summer drought dries up many waterfalls, and so there is little of the exuberant roar of water heard in every canyon when snows melt in spring, or the chatter of birds excited about their reproductive duties. In autumn, the summer tourist crowds have diminished, though hunters and sharpshooters, where allowed, may pepper the walls of ravines.

Autumn is a time of quiet and reflection, when the world is slowing down to receive the winter's blanket of snow and to freeze and silence the rambunctious cascades.

In the still-warm sun a few flowers burst out—azaleas, for example—as though they had the seasons reversed. But the days grow shorter, the nights more crisp. And in time the gathering clouds predict that winter is coming. These clouds may come as early as September, dropping immense amounts of moisture, filling the thirsty streambeds, soaking up soils, stirring the wildlife into action, and reactivating the roar of waterfalls.

But this does not last very long. Clouds swirl around the peaks for a while, and there may be a necklace of mist on the shoulders of a granite pinnacle. The deer seem to rejoice at this new and nearly forgotten excitement.

Yet the scene is no more secure than a veil of mist, and by morning the sun in a cloudless sky reminds all forms of life that the dryness of sumer and autumn continues.

Come December, storm clouds return, only this time they are deeper, blacker, wetter. They bring to the lower places curtains of rain, which fill the dry gullies and cause the rivers to roar again.

But in the high country the precipitation causes less violence, for the moisture turns to soft and nearly weightless flakes of fluffy snow, which build up to great depths. Each limb of oak, now bereft

Rime on grass

of leaves, collects a ridge of snow, and if the air is absolutely calm, these accumulations will reach a height of 4 inches before they tumble off.

With snow hip-deep on the ground, large fields of shrubbery and boulders disappear. The valleys and canyons assume a new dimension, possessed with all the paraphernalia of an Oz-like fantasy.

Seen on a clear morning after a snowstorm, the prevailing color is blue, for with the sun so low in the south, deeper canyons lie in dark blue shade. Fluffs of snow sift down from the bare oak limbs or slide off dark green conifer boughs.

Icicles glisten. On high peaks the wind begins to rise and after a while picks up great streams of loose snow and sends them off into the open air like giant banners in the sky. The snowbanks glitter with diamondlike points of light and turn all shades of yellow, orange, and purple with the passing day.

At this time of year the Pacific Crest Trail is largely engulfed in a massive weight of snow that, in some cases, scarcely melts even by the end of summer. A trek to Sierra Nevada summits in winter is less a matter of following any trail than of cross-country skiing to specific destinations from, say, existing ski developments. Conceivably one could follow the Pacific Crest Trail, but one would have to know it virtually by heart so as not to get lost. Anyway, it is not recommended. There are other ways to enjoy the mountains in winter.

One night we hiked along the Merced River as fog settled along the banks. Or was it rising from the water? A fog of any kind was unusual in these mountains. After a summer storm there may be mists or low clouds sifting through the trees. But they move, or swirl, or blow strongly with the canyon winds.

This winter fog lay quietly on the meadows and above the river. The air was still. The dry grass stalks stood motionless. Boughs of conifers hung as quietly as if they had frozen in place. With dusk, the light had nearly gone. The stream banks lay both blurred and dim. Yet something was happening in this strange milieu. We heard not a sound; the land was muffled. But the eerie air, so full of water, and the cushioned silence, meant at least that the mood was different. The stream had cloaked its shoulders in a shroud of grey. Everything solid seemed unsolid, unreal, shadowy, about to vanish.

Suddenly a faint glitter flicked through the gloom. How anything could be seen in light that faint we have no idea. But something along the river reflected what was surely the last vestige of daylight. At first we sensed it rather than saw it.

Flashlights were out in an instant. Nothing could be seen. No animal eyes. No fleeting fox. But there were a thousand "eyes."

Ice patterns in frozen pond

Down beside the water lay folded sheaves of grass and on each had formed minute crystals of ice.

We went closer. The fog, in freezing, had coated each strand with a string of ice needles. Along each blade the silvery fur of translucent white shone back at us, a gleaming cache of cold diamonds.

Here, all at once, created within minutes along the whole stream, and as temporary as a breath of warm wind, lay a sea of crystalline ice that could not have been fashioned by human hands in such intricate designs.

The temperature hovered at freezing. How many moments this masterpiece would last, we couldn't predict. A gust of wind could blow it away or a warm spell soften the needles into droplets.

The whole fantasy had come out of some darkening shroud and could evaporate before the hour. Few human beings would see it. Most people were either far from the mountains or unaware that such a miracle could appear before their eyes.

It was simply a crystallization of water from supersaturated air, the common process of rime formation. But here it lay in the Sierra, where an hour before we had had no hint of what was to happen. It was a miracle as major as the cellular structure of a leaf or the tracking instincts of a wolf.

Next morning the freeze had solidified. We went back. The rime had evaporated, but we found another legacy of the night. Though the river was running as merrily as ever through the rocks, little ponds and pondlets on the side lay frozen. Not solidly; the surface had sealed over, clasping needles of pine and boulders of granitic black and white. Press it slightly, and the icy crust would break.

The ice had frozen in translucent panes of varying thickness and opacity, in a series of overlapping geometric designs. That collection of angles, triangles, and curves was not repeated anywhere nearby, nor could it be redone even naturally. Every pond had frozen into a different pattern. Each morning a new palette would be offered. And most of the time there would be no eyes to appreciate it.

With the passing days, winter begins to change. There are two unmistakable signs of spring in the Sierra Nevada: the roar of rivers and falls, and the appearance of snow plants.

Even before the snow melts, vivid scarlet heads of snow plants come up through layers of needles, then through the snow and out into a cool wet world. There is no other plant in the Sierra Nevada that can be even remotely confused with snow plants. Their bright red overlapping leaves and abundant bell-shaped flowers are all so vivid that they can be spotted far through the woods, as though they were bits of fire.

A lack of chlorophyll makes the plant dependent not on photosynthesis to make its food but on dead organic matter. Thus it is very much like pinedrops and Indian pipes, two closely related members of the heath family.

Snow plants grow up to 18 inches tall and can be encountered at numerous places along the Pacific Crest Trail, especially in moist and sheltering woods.

Another sure sign of spring, or at least spring-to-come, is the march of flowers up out of the lowlands, week by week, to successively higher elevations. Millions of plants burst into bloom as the slopes are warmed, first with a greening, then a yellowing. California poppies, in association with tidy-tips, splash their color up the hills, and the effect is dazzling.

Redbud trees break out with strings of magenta flowers thickly clustered along their limbs. Dogwoods open up with a profusion that looks like snowfall in the forest. Azalea bushes become so thickly covered with white that they almost resemble a leftover snowbank. And on and on, up to the summits themselves.

The Sierra Nevada has well over 2,000 species of ferns and flowering plants, but many must hurry and reproduce in the time of spring rains, for beginning in March an austere brown creeps over the mountains. Sometimes there is little or no rain after February, save possibly a fall of snow in May. This means that the grasses, for example, must mature, produce their seeds, and turn to straw by midspring.

The melting snow pours icy waters over the cliffs, paints the walls with icicles, and brings on some rare phenomena. For example, if the air temperature drops considerably, the swiftly moving waters downstream from falls become choked with frazil ice. This happens when well-aerated water becomes so cold that spicules of ice form on its surface. These accumulating crystals may become so numerous that they clog the channel with a white slush that piles up from bank to bank and can even cause minor floods when the "ice jam" breaks.

On any one "capital excursion," as John Muir called his mountain ramblings, a hiker may not experience the entire march of seasons, but can certainly encounter different experiences in the course of a single day.

Midday is the least interesting time to be on the trail, biologically and photographically. Better to be out and looking, walking, contemplating at evening, night, or dawn. Long-distance hikers know this, but short-term or day travelers should take note and try to arrange their schedules so that they can spend their most valuable hours in the high country at dawn or dusk.

The alpen glow on ice and granite casts the whole Sierra Nevada into a golden or purple mood and lingers for more than an hour. At night, when the stars appear in dense and glittering clusters, the sky seems blacker and purer than ever. If there should be a moon, the stars are less intense in their display, but the granite peaks and banks of snow are bathed in an eerie light that is guaranteed to remain engraved in one's mind for years to come.

And if the stars are less intense at such times, we find another phenomenon—the moonbow. This resembles the rainbows one sees in spray of waterfalls during daytime, when solar radiation is broken up into colors of the spectrum. Seeing the same display in moonlit spray at such places as Yosemite Falls, or wherever the dancing waters eject their tissue of mist, is another memorable vision of a memorable mountain range.

6

Yosemite to Tahoe

The sense of the beautiful is God's best gift to the human soul.

W. H. Hudson, quoted by John
Galsworthy, in introduction to Hudson's
Green Mansions, 1916

THE MORNING MIST on Tuolumne Meadows is part of the pleasure of being out at dawn.

Lodgepole pines remain dark and gloomy at the fringes, as though a squadron of witches were winding slowly down from their nightly flights. Across grassy flats, peppered with little lodgepoles that seem to walk into the mist and disappear, a band of white cloud hangs over the curving stream of Tuolumne Creek. We see no movement—yet. The mist is stationary, though fragments of vapor sometimes sift up into the trees at the forest edge and evaporate above the treetops.

Suddenly one of the meadow's ghostly specks of lodgepole moves. Or at least it seems to move; the light is still poor. In a few moments we begin to see that not all the little trees are trees. One speck in particular stands a little higher than the others. It has a long neck, with a head down in the grass. In a moment the head comes up. A mule deer feeds at the edge of the fog.

There is no other movement, no sound except that of birds beginning to waken in the woods. The distant ridges remain dark blue, but the sky above them yellows. The undersides of the clouds turn silvery white, and faster than we can complete our examination of dawn, day has come.

The Pacific Crest Trail leaves Tuolumne Meadows in a north-

Desolation Wilderness

westerly direction, and once again surrounded by lodgepole pines, we hike through granite vales. Sharp-tipped peaks rise beyond the trees. Banks of purple lupine, with multiple stalks bearing clusters of sweet-pea-like flowers, line the path and recede in the shadows of narrow side streams that we must cross occasionally.

The river becomes larger, forming broad pools that are lined with grass, sand, or solid rock. The valley widens. We walk over bare granite composed of quartz and feldspar crystals, whitish or translucent, and crystals of dark minerals, such as mica, a sort of salt-and-pepper arrangement.

With a hand lens we make out the crystalline structure of this stone. Extraordinary scenes leap into view. The lens explores a confusion of shapes, yet finds an orderly arrangement, reflecting sunlight from geometrically shaped surfaces. What diamonds were ever handsomer? We have done as Emerson suggested: found the exquisite in the commonplace.

Coming to the brink of a ledge, we look into the wide amphitheater of Tuolumne Canyon, its walls largely barren domes, slopes, and cliffs, some gray, some stained with vertical lines of dark organic material. Trees spill down the gentle slopes in the distance, and even the baldest domes support lone pines that cling to some invisible crevice.

At Glen Aulin High Sierra Camp we turn north up Cold Canyon. Had we continued on down Tuolumne Canyon three miles, we would have passed some of the most dramatic waterfalls on earth, especially Waterwheel Falls. When the river is running full down this uneven incline, normally in July, the water strikes obstructions, flies 40 feet up into the air, and spins around, an endlessly rotating sheet of white spray. For a mile the water plunges violently down this slope with a roar that echoes from wall to wall of the canyon.

Proceeding north from Glen Aulin and then west, the Pacific Crest Trail zigs and zags as it descends into one canyon after another, comes up over ridges, curves past lakes, and then turns north along Falls Creek to the northern border of Yosemite National Park.

In a region of granite the trail goes along the eastern edge of the Emigrant Wilderness, a 98,000-acre reserve that rises to an elevation of 11,570 feet on the summit of Leavitt Peak. More than a hundred lakes are scattered throughout the wilderness, a typical Sierra Nevada scene.

But here the mountains begin to change. Soon we shall leave those polished domes and undulating slopes bearing glacially scattered boulders. Volcanic country is ahead, and an introduction to the coarse, dark brown lava so familiar north of here is to be found in the Emigrant Wilderness. We also begin to see the mountain hemlock more often, a tree that covers the Pacific Crest Trail much of the way between here and Canada.

This wilderness was named for emigrants who came through during Gold Rush days. The first wagon group over the pass was a party consisting of W. J. Duckwall, his wife and six children, John and Si Murphy, a man named Collins, and two ox-drawn wagons. In 1853, after struggling for 1,500 miles across desert country, the emigrants were confronted by the enormous barrier of the Sierra Nevada. Perplexed and bewildered as to how to get across, they fell prey to Captain J. W. Patrick, who has otherwise gone down in history as the second mayor of the town of Sonora. Patrick, ever loyal to his community, patrolled the Carson River for the apparent purpose of steering emigrants across the Sierra on a route that would take them through Sonora. He did this by telling weary travelers how hazardous all other routes were: for example, how they lay strewn with the victims of landslides and Indian attacks. By comparison, the Emigrant Trail to Sonora must have seemed like a broad boulevard.

The group was finally persuaded to go the Sonora route, but as things turned out, it was good for Captain Patrick that they never saw him again. For the route was anything but easy. The wagons had to be lifted by hand over innumerable obstacles. Cattle wandered off and the emigrants had to round them up in formidable mountain terrain. They could never tell when the first snows would fall and maroon them in the mountains. Or when hostile Indians would open fire. On September 27 the party managed to struggle over the pass, but the last few miles down to Relief Station on the west side were dangerous and precipitous. The group arrived with wrecked wagons, splintered yokes, broken chains, and despair that must have been tempered only by the fact that they all made it alive.

By the time hikers arrive at Sonora Pass they are walking steadily on lava, leaving the Sierra Nevada behind. However, they will still see those two familiar trees of the Sierra crests: lodgepole and whitebark pines. At first these species are difficult to tell apart, as they mingle and appear somewhat alike in Sonora Pass. But after a while the observer begins to see that the whitebark's cones are longer, bark is whiter, needles more flexible and more abundant per cluster, and the young trunks have a smoother surface. The whitebark also tends to grow in clumps, whereas the lodgepole is often solitary. Unlike the cones of any other North American pine, the cones of whitebark break up while still on the tree, and would fall to the ground scale by scale if chipmunks and Clark's nutcrackers did not tear them apart to get at the seeds.

The whitebark is principally an indicator of high altitudes and

Sierra juniper, Carson Pass

grows most often in bouldery places. It may not grow very much each year. A whitebark three hundred years old may be but 4 feet tall. Its tenacity in the face of searing icy winds, intense solar radiation, and extremes of drought is indicative of enormous staying power.

A recurring delight along the Pacific Crest Trail is close-up examination of small ecosystems. No two are alike. None has the same music or fragrance as another. Each holds surprises, and the closer we look the more we discover. These little habitats delay us as much as anything else.

For example, in Sonora Pass a tiny side stream comes barely trickling over the lava. You cannot hear its delicate glissandos without getting close, and then you must duck under the willows into which it disappears and crouch in a cool "mini-ravine."

Compared to semiarid sagebrush fields beyond the banks of the gully, this world is completely different, filled with moisture and greenness. Within this diminutive glen, shrubs of currant bloom with inconspicuous red and yellow flowers as they drape over a small moss-coated ledge. Penstemons poke out of small crevices. Fallen leaves and needles sifted down through the willow canopy lie askew in the tangled maze of vegetation. Lupines attempt to grow up through this mat of living matter. Amid the multiple stems we pick out monkey flower, shooting star, iris, sedge, and grass. So strong is the aroma of mint in the air that there must be pennyroyal around.

A little snow remains, sculptured, trenched, melting slowly. The tiny hollow is filled with liquid music from the stream. We drink—and could not find purer water. Indeed, we suddenly realize that we have entered a pure and unsullied world. For the moment it belongs to us and no one else. We disturb nothing and take nothing, except inspiration. We cannot quite explain it but we feel recharged.

Along the trail there are thousands of such green mansions if we know where to look for them and how to appreciate their solitude. W. H. Hudson, in his own *Green Mansions*, said that the sweetest thing solitude has for us is that we are free in it; no convention holds us.

Northwest of Ebbetts Pass the Pacific Crest Trail enters the Mokelumne Wilderness, a 50,450-acre wild area encompassing the upper tributaries of the Mokelumne River. Great masses of granite comprise the higher regions, sprinkled sparsely with twisted, wind-battered junipers. The streams run southwesterly, through deep canyons they have cut in the rock.

There is a great deal of tumbling, too, for within this wilderness the elevation drops from Mokelumne Peak, at 9,371 feet, to the

Mokelumne River canyon at 4,000 feet. In scattered forests the hiker soon appreciates the noble qualities of two trees: giant red fir, with its russet trunk and soft luxuriant foliage, and silver pine, with rich red bark broken into square or rectangular plates.

The mountain hemlock is easily identified by its drooping branches and nodding tip, and we could study the intricate contortions and coloration of Sierra junipers for hours. These trees are either lodged in protected swales or rooted in crevices on exposed promontories. But they are little more conspicuous than sulfur-yellow patches of buckwheat, which brighten the mountains in exposed as well as protected habitats.

The Pacific Crest Trail descends to the Mokelumne River, then climbs 4,000 feet past delightful Summit City Canyon and Fourth of July Lake, in due course reaching Carson Pass and California Highway 88.

It was in the Carson Pass area during 1844 that John C. Fremont, with Kit Carson as scout, made the first recorded winter crossing of the Sierra Nevada, the first recorded ascent of an identifiable peak in that range, and the first recorded mention of Lake Tahoe.

It seems incredible that scarcely five years after these events California was descended upon by one of the greatest mass immigrations in history. The 1848 discovery of gold at Sutter's Mill, about 60 miles west of the Pacific Crest Trail at this point, transformed the Sierra Nevada from Indian territory to white man's country in a few years. As we look back the past century or so, we see that the population swelled from about 255,000 persons to more than 20 million today.

Such an explosion is certainly readily explained by the attraction of gold. And there was indeed gold in the mountains, some of it solid in veins, some in great chunks, some concentrated in gravels where gold had washed like pebbles down the canyons and out of the mountains.

Neither hardship nor disappointment nor backbreaking travel and work—little but death stopped the early gold seeker in his desperate, frenzied search for sudden wealth. Few phenomena so short-lived have made such an impact on history. Buried treasure brought out every vice of greedy men, every humor, pathos, joy, success, defeat. The California Gold Rush lasted less than a decade, but it was intense enough that analyses of it have filled volumes.

What is left? The gold is gone, except for that which is still locked in the rock. The sluice gates have long since rotted away or washed downstream. Shacks and sheds have vanished as permanently as the California grizzly. Shouts, jokes, singing, fandangos, howls of glee, wails of woe—all these are mere echoes. And Lotta Crabtree? Black Bart?

Remote pond in Desolation Wilderness

Dust. But dust is universe-building. We can reconstruct, in the saloons left over from that or later eras, the brawls and violence when miners hit town a-rarin'; we can read of the wild gaiety and imagine the doings in town. But out among the rocks and in deep ravines we are closest to the hardrock miner himself and can perhaps see his true character: lonely, forlorn, forgotten, broke.

To the Pacific Crest Trail hiker looking down upon these hills and canyons where much of it happened, the pursuit of gold may seem like some nadir of American history, comprehensible only by placing oneself in that era.

Along the trail, or within a short distance from it, may be found historic remains from those mining and settling years. History buffs can become very much absorbed because there are maps, books, restored towns, and wayside exhibits that bring back some of the pioneer era.

An illuminating side trip can be made to old Columbia, a mining town located near Sonora and now reconstructed and furnished with one of the finest collections of historic artifacts in the mountains. It is about 40 miles west of the Pacific Crest Trail, but a hiker who can get to it will have a new appreciation of the mining era at its height in the 1850s. Its lively exhibits and activities make it somewhat of a Williamsburg of the West. Other towns with mining aura still intact include Angels Camp, Mokelumne Hill, Coloma (where Sutter's Mill is located), Placerville, and Oroville.

Along the trail north of Echo Pass, in the Desolation Wilderness, are few minerals of value, and so this region is not mining country itself, but it lies between the Comstock Lode to the east and the Mother Lode to the west, and has been the scene of exploration as well as cross-country travel by frantic gold seekers. Hundreds of wagons made the grueling trip over Echo Summit until 1868, when a railroad was built across the Sierra Nevada 40 miles north of here.

The Desolation Wilderness, established by Congress in 1969, has long been protected by the United States Forest Service for hiking, camping, and related types of recreation in a wilderness environment. Ironically, its name originally referred to the open, seemingly desolate Sierra highlands here, which are as magnificent as any; but human beings caused more desolation than nature did.

In 1875 a dam was constructed, then its height raised in 1917. According to Robert S. Wood, whose *Desolation Wilderness* is an excellent guide to the 200 miles of trails and 139 trout streams and lakes here, "the dam transformed a series of small lakes (Medley Lakes) in the shallow polished granite basin into the giant and ill-named Aloha. In the fall when the water is let out, the basin becomes a desolate scene of cracked mud and drowned snags."

Worse yet, a dam was constructed on the Rubicon River in

1957, transforming Onion Flat into a reservoir. A tunnel drilled through the rock carried water into Rockbound Lake. Then another dam converted this lake into a reservoir and another tunnel was drilled to transfer the runoff from Rockbound Valley into Loon Lake.

With all this manipulation of the natural features, one would hardly expect the wilderness to retain much of its original charm. But Wood himself calls Desolation country the gentlest, friendliest, most inviting section of the Sierra Nevada crest.

It is also the most accessible. On the south, U.S. Route 50 goes over Echo Summit, less than four hours' drive from the San Francisco Bay area. As a result, thousands upon thousands of hikers and campers have spread out across the area for years, and the Desolation has become severely trampled. Trails are numerous but mostly unsigned, so it is not uncommon to see a perplexed hiker poring over a map and wondering where the trail is. True wilderness never had signs, however, and one should not expect the Forest Service to clutter this area by trying to sign the complex trail network.

Rather, hikers should be on their own. If those following the Pacific Crest Trail would like to spend a few days on side trails, they should equip themselves with special maps and guidebooks.

The same is true for day-hikers going in from any other entrance. We went in the hard way—by old road from Lake Tahoe and Fallen Leaf Lake, thence up an all-but-abandoned trail that called for scrambling across loose rock and plowing through brush up a 2,000-foot incline.

Starting out on this track, we realized that we were not supposed to stray off the trail, because Private Property and No Trespassing signs ornamented the path. Farther on, these diminished and disappeared and we noticed a number of MacGillivray's warblers flying about in the shrubbery. Wrens and robins also kept us company. Through dense vegetation and past large patches of paintbrush the trail led into forests of lodgepole and Jeffrey pines. We hopped across streams and entered fern-clogged dells where bright orange tiger lilies bloomed.

Beyond Grass Lake we began to ascend steeply, and the way became more rocky and rough. But this lifted us out of the valley and we got finer views of fir-covered ridges, hidden lakes, and patches of snow. The higher we climbed the more we encountered Townsend's solitaires and Steller's jays. Wild roses grew head high.

Wherever we found some barren rock, it usually showed polish or grooves from glacial action. The mountains seemed jumbled, broken, disconnected, discolored, and we walked at times on sharp broken plates of rock, very likely split in the process of freezing and thawing each year.

Mountain mahogany

But we also passed through soft mountain glades where wild delphiniums and phlox held forth. When mountain hemlocks became abundant with juncos chattering in their branches, we knew we were close to the Canadian life zone.

Small streams fell over rocks and rotting logs on their way down the ridge. Stream banks burgeoned with yellow monkey flowers and lay under a drapery of lupine, grass, and heather. Near the top we came to a sheltered meadow awash in a sea of lupine.

And not long after that, climbing over a shelf of ragged rock, we reached Lucille Lake. Circled by pines, anchored on one side by cliffs, this quiet pond seemed made for artists, photographers, campers, and swimmers. Old logs lay half submerged in grass at the water's edge, and beyond them reflections from patches of snow on the rocks above appeared to illuminate the depths with a kind of diffused incandescence.

We walked farther and found more lakes, stepped into fern-filled glens, climbed through hemlock woods to upper ridges, descended to lakes at the base of the Crystal Range.

Along the way we passed one of the handsomest offerings made by nature in the Sierra Nevada: a field of pussy-paws in bloom. The color was like no other—a reddish-salmon-orange-purple mix of rounded blossoms that seldom lifted very far above the ground. This gave the appearance of a matted carpet, but the ground was hot and dry. Pussy-paws, in the purslane family, grows from dry dusty earth; it is so rugged and tenacious that it can hold its own despite summer drought and high temperatures from the nearly unfiltered sun.

Bees hovered over this bonanza of blossoms. We caught a faint aroma of mint and saw some of the other flourishing species: orange and yellow paintbrush, phlox, lupine, buckwheat. We remembered patches of pussy-paws south along the Pacific Crest Trail, but this massed concentration on a high ridge showed us as well as anything that the Desolation Wilderness is hardly desolate.

Trails in this area are generally free of snow, and the fords are wadable by July. August is least encumbered by snow, but hikers wishing to avoid the crowds should stay away during late summer. At times, mosquitoes are a serious problem, so repellent should be carried.

Views from the summits of peaks are, of course, magnificent, with Lake Tahoe dominating the landscape to the east. Although much Desolation high country is open and treeless, other environments are reached by side trails: secluded dells, wooded canyons, dramatic cliffs, marshes, meadows, roaring waterfalls, wild rivers, and countless lakes. Throughout the area it is possible to see deer, coyotes, golden eagles, and numerous forms of smaller wildlife.

From Echo Summit into Echo Lakes Basin and Desolation Valley, then above Fallen Leaf Lake and through the western part of the Velma Lakes Basin, the Pacific Crest Trail makes its closest approach to Lake Tahoe—about 4 miles.

Situated in a faulted basin whose outlet was dammed by volcanic activity, Lake Tahoe measures 12 by 22 miles, with a maximum depth of 1,658 feet. People sensitive to natural beauty have expressed dismay at what has happened to this once pristine lake and its environs. The basin, since the early 1950s, has been subjected to new roads, ski areas, and multiple commercial projects by developers and gaming interests. Among the consequences have been silt and raw sewage discharged into some of the purest waters on earth, and the production of algal scum that eventually leads to the death of lakes.

Changes to the lakeshore were so extensive that by the 1970s only 41 percent of the vegetation around the lake remained in its natural state. Transmission lines and billboards proliferated, and more than a dozen species of wildlife in the region had to be listed by the Forest Service as endangered. Smog in the basin became so thick that fire lookouts were canceled because observers could not have seen forest fires if there had been any. Today, however, the Forest Service is undertaking a campaign to clean up and protect more of the Lake Tahoe surroundings, so it is hoped that the trend will be reversed.

Leaving Desolation Wilderness, the trail passes through dense forests, meadows, and open slopes of sagebrush and aspen. The elevations become lower, for at last we leave the Sierra Nevada. Our way is through incense cedar, Jeffrey pine and white fir at elevations down toward 6,000 feet.

At times the hiking can be hot and dusty along dry ridges, and we dare not refill our canteens in contaminated lakes. But perseverance, and a water container of adequate size, will get us through.

Winter in this area is a time of exceptionally heavy snows, and the celebrated Squaw Valley lies some 3 miles east of the Pacific Crest Trail. This recreation area, site of the 1960 Winter Olympics, receives about 450 inches of snow a year. The site has 29 lifts, a hotel, motels, shops, and other facilities that are still very much in operation. Squaw Valley, once a California state recreation area, has been sold to private developers and attracts nearly a million visitors a year.

The Pacific Crest Trail, away from the crowds, subdivisions, and traffic jams of Squaw Valley, continues along the headwaters of the American River to the west. Less than 10 miles away is the wild 3,000-foot-deep gorge of the North Fork of the river, conserved within Tahoe National Forest.

As we walk along enjoying the remote solitude, it is hard to imagine that to the early immigrants the wilderness was sometimes anything but joyous. It could be savage, hostile, fearsome, deadly—especially to inexperienced pioneers arriving from the east, exhausted after weeks of unrelenting hardships on the desert.

Such was the Donner Party which started from Illinois in 1846, barely ahead of the great influx of gold seekers. The Donners were not miners but simply immigrants with much more experience farming than surviving wilderness rigors.

Other people were leaving the east, too, and by the time the Donners arrived in California their group had grown into a train of 87 persons.

In late October they found themselves trapped by heavy snow while attempting to cross the Sierra Nevada. Cabins were hastily constructed. Crude shelters of brush and canvas were put up in desperate efforts to shut out the elements.

But the snow fell, eventually to a depth of 22 feet, and the poor souls had to spend the winter where they were. The story is much told and widely known, and we need only summarize it as a reminder that hardships of modern times pale beside those of the early travelers in these mountains.

The party planned to kill and eat their cattle, but most of these wandered away in a storm. One man killed a grizzly bear; no other large animals were seen. The marooned victims had no traps to catch smaller wildlife, and even if they had, there wouldn't have been enough animals in the vicinity to supply so large a group of people.

As starvation took its toll, the survivors had to eat dogs, hides, and even the flesh of their dead companions.

Some members of the party finally got across the pass on improvised snowshoes. Rescue parties saved the rest the following spring. But only 47 persons survived. The remaining 40 had perished.

The Pacific Crest Trail hiker who wants to visit the site of the tragedy will find Donner Memorial State Park located 5 miles east of the trail route in Donner Pass. The park has exhibits, campsites, picnic areas, and water recreation activities on Donner Lake.

A happier and more successful group to pioneer this area just after the Donner group was the Mormon Battalion. In 1846 the United States and Mexico went to war over California after the Mexicans refused to sell the territory to the United States. One group of soldiers enlisted in the cause was called the Mormon Battalion. These men marched south through Santa Fe to California but got there too late to fight (the war ended in 1848).

The Mormons were discharged and took what jobs they could find before returning to Utah. Some were at Sutter's Mill when gold was discovered there. Some were heading back east via Donner Pass when they received word to spend the winter in California, so they waited and set out again when spring came.

On July 19, 1848, the Battalion, consisting of forty-five men and one woman, left Placerville, California, with 17 wagons, 150 horses, and about 150 cattle. A few miles en route they discovered the bodies of three scouts they had sent ahead—murdered and robbed by the Indians. They called the place Tragedy Springs, a name that still survives.

Building road as they went, they reached the pass by July 28. They had an advantage in trail building over anyone coming across the mountains in the opposite direction: they were all, people and domestic animals, fresh and well fed, and the geography was to their advantage. The ridges coalesced going upslope so that once they got on a ridge they could stay there.

Within weeks they completed their crossing, a feat of road-opening for which they never received due credit in their own time.

Lassen Peak

7

Lava Country

*The hours hurry by with singular
swiftness. Minutes or miles are nothing.*

Clarence King, *Mountaineering in the
Sierra Nevada*, 1872

AFTER THE ROARING traffic on six-lane Interstate 80 through Donner
Pass, plus gasoline stations, ski developments, restaurants, and motels, it is pleasant to get back among the pines, firs, and hemlocks.

Not far northwest of Donner Pass the Pacific Crest Trail enters
the drainage of the Yuba River. The land is less rugged than the
Sierra Nevada crest to which we have become accustomed, with
more low ridges and broad meadows surrounded by lodgepole pines.
Unless one is an accomplished botanist it may not be possible to
recognize all the plants, but aster, senecio, and sedge are abundant
in much of the United States.

The hiker will become well acquainted with corn lily in the
next few hundred miles. This plant is also known both as false
hellebore and, unfortunately, as skunk cabbage, but it is distinctly
unlike either the eastern or western skunk cabbages. It grows in
wet places and meadows between low elevations and high mountain
passes from California north through Washington. The twisted arms
of the plant, shaggy with flowers, rise two or three feet. The roots
and young shoots contain veratridine, an alkaloid poisonous to livestock; hence the plants are seldom eaten. The flowers are said to be
poisonous to insects and sometimes kill great numbers of honeybees.
The plant graces many a mile of the trail, its large leaves twisted
into shapes that look like green waves at sea.

The streams now seem to meander rather than crash or cascade,

133

and in the curving loops there are gentle sun-flecked glades as grand and colorful as the most carefully cultured gardens. Orange lilies glow like bursts of fire. Monkshoods lift their royal velvet blooms on stalks 3 feet tall. A flash of lavender comes from wild delphinium. Yellow monkey flowers hug the banks.

Among the flowers and in and out of the shadows a sky-blue butterfly undulates in flashing flight. If we probe too near the stream, a frog leaps off the bank and plunges into the water. That chirping chatter in the woods comes from juncos, and the calls at the edges of meadows are emitted by flycatchers. On a tree stump, the kestrel silently oversees these events, doubtless watching for some careless meadow mouse to emerge from hiding. We hear a song sparrow in the distance and glimpse warblers and kinglets.

It is difficult to walk very far without crossing the path of a golden-mantled ground squirrel or seeing the tracks of deer. These animals do not come near us, but with mosquitoes we have an intimate acquaintance.

Crossing a country road, we are startled by the sight of a station wagon carrying a boat on top and pulling a trailer with a motorcycle on back. We muse over how little we require as hikers to enjoy *our* environment. To be out where we can stop and observe great thunderheads building up in the afternoon and hear the songs of meadowlarks is entertainment, recreation, and inspiration combined. We do not tire of it because there is always something new. We do not need supplementary vehicles in pursuit of life, liberty, and happiness.

All we need is an extra hour or two each day.

Descending into the Yuba River drainage area, the trail passes through dense deciduous forests characteristic of lower elevations: bigtooth maple with its rich-green, deeply cleft leaves; mountain alder overhanging the rushing waters; a patch of black oaks; scattered cottonwoods.

The Yuba River is also gold country—or was. Some of the lower streams were altered in the days of hydraulic mining, when high-powered jets of water brought down the softer hillsides, clogged the streams with silt, and wiped out native aquatic life.

Up here, the streams have been spared human rapaciousness, and the music of their leaping from boulder to boulder and pool to pool fills the canyon. The Yuba and its tributaries now serve recreationists more than miners, and the natural beauty is likely to be admired longer than the gold.

With fresh aromas from aquatic environments along the stream, we think we have left the Sierra Nevada behind, but suddenly we are confronted by dazzling crags and towers of the Sierra Buttes.

These sharp-edged summits are part of a massif made up of both volcanic and sedimentary rocks, its glacial basins filled with lakes. The cliffs rise abruptly from the banks of the Yuba River near Sierra City and soar nearly 4,000 feet above the trail. The hiker is fortunate to see the dramatic, plunging ridges and amphitheaters on this eastern side; from the west there is no precipitous rise, but rather a gentle descent from the summit.

The Sierra Buttes are seen long before they are reached—and as we climb up out of the Yuba River canyon, heading over a divide and along a ridge to the north, they constitute a landmark behind us, conspicuous for being so Sierra-like in a region more subdued.

We now come to a cluster of charming blue lakes set in a bowl of deep fir forests. Lakes Basin deserves a day of exploration if one can manage it. The sun comes up at six on summer mornings and illuminates the fir groves like cathedral naves aglow with light from stained glass windows.

It is quiet and breezeless. A spot of sun falls on wolf lichen clinging to a tree trunk, and the whole grove seems momentarily to radiate with a halo of yellow-green. This lichen, so common in northern California, is well known for its prevalence in redwood groves. There on rusty brown trunks and here on the dark red bark of fir and incense cedar, it clings and gives the forest a spotted aspect. For photographers it adds a special touch of color.

A deer is up, browsing in the forest. Chipmunks skitter through the undergrowth. A marmot scampers into a patch of willows.

Most of the sounds are faint. A stream sings softly beyond the edge of the woods. Bumblebees gather around a clump of mint.

The hiker does not tarry too long in the shadows; anyone who pauses is fair game for mosquitoes.

There are glades with giant columns of fir festooned with lichen, and around each trunk young firs grow by the dozens. The forest floor is covered with bearberry and mats of pine and fir needles.

The day lengthens. Shadows shorten. Breezes rise. Out in the meadows, grasses grow head high; they seem to burst out, reaching skyward as if in defiance of the competing trees, or springing up rapidly after the weight of 10 to 20 feet of snow has been released each winter.

Suddenly, catching the light just right, we see up against the shadows of tree walls skeins of spider webs sailing on the breeze. They are nearly invisible, reflecting only the merest glint of sunlight. Some blow out over the meadow and disappear. Some fall among the grasses. Some soar from tree to tree. Altogether it looks as though slender strands of sunlight were flying across the meadows.

Now we come to a small pond whose surface ripples with an incoming stream of water. Beyond this we have to pick our way with care among volcanic boulders.

On treeless sites shrubby forms of oak and manzanita crouch among the rocks, never failing to grow, it seems, where other species would have a difficult time. Nature's empty niches do not remain empty very long. The land is not to be open forever; young firs and lodgepole pines have sprung up. The place looks very much like the site of some previous forest fire.

The music grows in crescendo. Calls of warblers, sparrows, and finches fill the woods. Through the trees come the celestial notes of a veery. Bees around the mint patches have multiplied and sound like a chorus. Grasshoppers flip noisily across the path.

Spots of red come into view: paintbrush, gilia, penstemon, snow plant; the last has begun to shrivel, its scarlet less bright than usual.

The day becomes dry and hot, but at little oases where tiny streams trickle, great numbers of birds and butterflies gather.

Back on the Pacific Crest Trail, we look down into Lakes Basin and see the lakes placed as though pieces of sky had been detached and scattered among the trees.

We asked local people what they thought of the Pacific Crest Trail going past their region, and they noted, with a touch of sadness, that although the Trail is a much-admired asset, it is also much abused.

"We're having troubles with vandalism," said one resident. "No sooner does the Forest Service complete a section of the trail than vandals move in to pull up the signs, relocate them, or throw them away."

"Trail bikes are also troublesome," another resident told us. "Everyone knows that motorized vehicles are not permitted on the trail—but you see the tracks. In winter, snowmobiles are a problem. Parties come in and go wherever they please, rules or no rules, trail or no trail."

Shortly after entering Plumas County, we pass near Plumas-Eureka State Park—one of the prime surprises along the Pacific Crest Trail. It is famous not only as an early mining site where many of the facilities are still intact, but as the birthplace of competitive skiing in the Western Hemisphere.

The mining aspects happen to be well preserved indeed. The park lies on Jamison Creek, 5 miles southwest of Blairsden, California, and includes Eureka Peak, where rich veins of gold-bearing rock were discovered in 1851.

For more than two decades the Eureka Lode became a center of mining activities. The quiet valley turned into a noisy, lively place, what with grinding stones crushing ore, blacksmiths repairing wagons or shoeing horses, stamp mills going full volume, and waterwheels creaking and turning to supply power.

At one time three overhead tramways operated up the moun-

Corn lily

tainside, carrying ore in huge buckets from the Eureka Tunnel, which eventually reached back into the mountain for more than a mile.

The work of bringing out ore was not easy or safe. Men were mangled by machinery, run over by ore carts, and buried by cave-ins. Elsewhere, they had to contend with grizzly bears, which shared the mountains with them.

In the towns, several forms of entertainment were available to the miners, and there must have been much spirits-induced conviviality. Old-timers could remember the time in Jamison City when Black Bart shot Spanish Pete. Tong wars erupted among the Chinese. According to local reports, it was not unusual to see four fist fights at once on Saturday night in the main street.

Then in winter came a new excitement. Skiing (referred to in those days as snow-shoeing) developed into an organized sport on account of the abundant snow and the residents' need for outdoor recreation. The first ski clubs and annual competitions were organized in 1861 in the mining towns of Whiskey Diggings, Poker Flat, Port Wine, Onion Valley, La Porte, Jamison City, and Johnsville. Before long other towns joined in the fun, sent forth their own champion skiers, and held local meets nearly every weekend.

"Snow-Shoe Races!" the posters announced. "Four days snowshoe racing at Howland Flat, under the auspicies of the Table Rock Snow-Shoe Club." The poster went on to describe a program of dances all week and a grand ball on St. Patrick's night.

To keep the snow from sticking to their crude skis, the contestants experimented with sperm candle, oil, tallow, varnish, shoe wax, pitch, balsam, turpentine, camphor, and oil of cedar. From these efforts came a concoction called Sierra Lightning, mixed and cooked by "dopemen" with secret methods that insured effectiveness on just about any kind of snow.

It must have worked. One contestant managed a speed of 88 miles an hour on a short run. Aside from the glamour of competitive skiing, there were people whose daily work required great skiing prowess; one still hears talk of Snowshoe Thompson, who carried mail over the mountains for years.

Today, skiing is still a winter pastime here: facilities in Plumas-Eureka State Park include a ski lift and warming hut. Visitors may also examine the stamp mill, powder house, blacksmith shop, stable, ore carts and other paraphernalia of the mining era. But the clanking at the mines and the shouting of the miners is history, which we recall as we wander among the remains of a society that thrived more than a century ago.

We are now in the drainage of the celebrated Feather River, a rugged canyon country that has here and there been tamed by roads and reservoirs. Miners clawed their way up into these rugged regions and even found one of the world's largest gold nuggets (54 pounds).

The middle fork is today the wildest; it was designated in 1968 as a National Wild River. To descend into it, hikers must negotiate steep switchbacks that bring them down to around 3,000 feet elevation—good country for flies, heat, and rattlesnakes. But there is also an escape: one can take a refreshing swim in the river.

Pacific Crest Trail hikers are not likely to be carrying the kind of equipment needed to negotiate precipitous cliffs and ravines in this country, so they should take special care on side explorations.

The trail proceeds through dense forest, rises, and then descends again, this time into the canyon of the North Fork of the Feather River. This best-known fork, traversed by rail and highway, offers attractive views where not clear-cut or discolored by air-dropped fire retardants.

Once more we are in the heart of gold-mining country. The sand and gravel bars that formed along meanders of these rivers were logical sites for concentration of free gold, and it did not take the early miners long to discover that. They stampeded into the mountains, disregarding the remoteness and lack of supplies, found gold in abundance, and swarmed over the bars like digging ants.

The Pacific Crest Trail passes near Rich Bar, one of the most renowned localities, with a double claim to fame. Five miles upstream from the trail crossing, it was the site of the largest gold strike in the Feather River canyon, and in its heyday yielded up some $20 million in gold.

Though a population of more than 2,500 once lived there, the evidence today has all but vanished. However, we know more of what went on at Rich Bar than we know about any other mining camp in the Gold Rush era. This is owing to a series of letters written there under the nom de plume of Dame Shirley (Mrs. Louise Amelia Clappe), the intelligent, well-bred wife of a mountain doctor. Her letters covered only a year (1851–52) but they tell of the raw and rugged social life of the miners and conditions at a mining camp, and are considered one of the best eyewitness accounts of the period.

She wrote of her trip up into the mountains:

> I wish I could give you some faint idea of the majestic solitudes through which we passed, where the pine trees rise so grandly in their awful height, that they seem looking into Heaven itself. . . . It was worth the whole wearisome journey, danger from Indians, grizzly bears, sleeping under the stars, and all, to behold this beautiful vision. While I stood breathless with admiration, a singular sound and an exclamation of "A

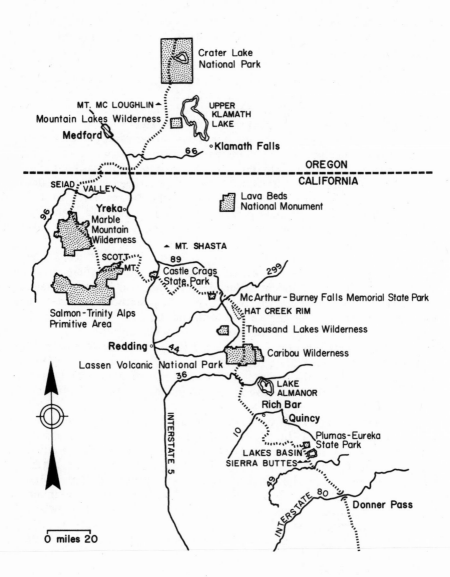

THE PACIFIC CREST TRAIL IN NORTHERN CALIFORNIA

rattlesnake!" . . . startled me into common sense again. I gave one look at the reptile, horribly beautiful, like a chain of living opals,—as it cork-screwed itself into that peculiar spiral, which it is compelled to assume in order to make an attack, and then fear overcoming curiosity—although I had never seen one of them before—I galloped out of its vicinity, as fast as my little mule could carry me.

Dame Shirley was widely praised by the male population of Rich Bar because of her courage and fortitude in coming so far into the wilderness. But she said that she was "particularly careful all the time not to inform my admirers that my courage was the result of the know nothing, fear nothing principle."

The importance of Rich Bar as a mining spot was described by her, starting from the first discovery.

In a fortnight from that time, the two men who found the first bit of gold had each taken out six thousand dollars. Two others took out thirty-three pounds of gold in eight hours; which is the best day's work that has been done on this branch of the river; the largest amount ever taken from one panful of dirt was fifteen hundred dollars. In little more than a week after its discovery, five hundred men had settled upon the bar for the summer.—Such is the wonderful alacrity with which a mining town is built.

The living quarters of the residents of Rich Bar can well be imagined, especially from this comment: "I must mention that the floor is so uneven that no article of furniture gifted with four legs pretends to stand upon but three at once, so that the chairs, tables, etc., remind you constantly of a dog with a sore foot."

The law of the time was typical mountain justice, but Dame Shirley was wholly understanding toward the miners. "A more generous, hospitable, intelligent and industrious people, than the inhabitants of the half-dozen Bars—of which Rich Bar is the nucleus— never existed; for you know how proverbially wearing it is to the nerves of manhood, to be entirely without either occupation or amusement; and that has been pre-eminently the case during the present month."

The month was January, 1852, and she was describing the cooped-up condition of the community:

Imagine a company of enterprising and excitable young men, settled upon a sandy level, about as large as a poor widow's potato patch, walled in by sky-kissing hills—absolutely *compelled* to remain, on account of the weather, which has vetoed indefinitely their Exodus—with no place to ride or drive, even if they had the necessary vehicles and quadrupeds,—with no newspapers or politics to interest them,—deprived of all books but a few dog-eared novels of the poorest class,—churches, lectures, lyceums, theaters and (most unkindest cut of all!) pretty girls, having become to these unhappy men myths,—without *one* of the thousand ways of passing time peculiar to civilization,—most of them living in damp, gloomy cabins, where Heaven's dear light can enter only by the door,—and, when you add to all these disagreeables the fact that, during the never-to-be-forgotten month, the most remorseless, persevering rain which ever set itself to work to drive humanity mad, has been pouring doggedly down, sweeping away bridges, lying in uncomfortable puddles about nearly all the habitations, wickedly insinuating itself beneath un-umbrella-protected shirt-collars, generously treating to a shower-bath *and* the rheumatism sleeping bipeds, who did not happen to have an Indian-rubber blanket,—and, to crown all, rendering mining utterly impossible,—you cannot wonder that even the most moral should have become somewhat reckless.

Dame Shirley describes their recklessness, "Saturnalias," and other aspects of personal life under adverse conditions, and her letters make fascinating reading and reference.

Under such conditions as she described, it is sometimes difficult to understand why so many people stayed so long. Surely the potential of the mountain's yielding great riches kept them on, but there were few surprises. "Gold mining is Nature's great lottery scheme," Dame Shirley said. "A man may work in a claim for many months, and be poorer at the end of the time than when he commenced; or he may 'take out' thousands in a few hours. It is a mere matter of chance. A friend of ours . . . a person of intelligence and education, told us that, after 'working a claim' for six months, he had taken out but six ounces."

Dame Shirley came regretfully down from the mountains. She liked the "wild and barbarous life," the beauty of the river, and the firs. Her principal summation of the experience was as suitable for her times as it is today appropriate for the Pacific Crest Trail hiker: "Really, everybody ought to go to the mines, just to see how little it takes to make people comfortable in the world."

A few people still make something of a living by mining gold in these mountains. Some work part time, some full time, some with partners, some without. Occasionally miners can be seen attired in rubber suits and diving gear, descending into pools, ponds, and lakes, where they sometimes find nuggets as big as their thumbs.

Coming up out of the Feather River canyon, the Pacific Crest Trail heads north across volcanic terrain, through coniferous forests west of Almanor Reservoir.

We are leaving the lands of the Maidu, northernmost of the original Sierra Nevada Indians. These people occupied the foothills, and some lived year round in the sheltered mountain valleys of Feather River country. Hunters, trappers, traders, fishermen, gatherers, they depended on their surroundings for a living and had not only respect but reverence for wild things.

Acorns were their staff of life, but they ate or used a great many other products of nature. They painted and tattooed their skin, wore their hair long, and ornamented themselves—though at times they wore little or no clothing. The winter house was a partly subterranean circular lodge, but the people also occupied lean-tos of bark and brush. Maidus made stone tools and excelled in basketry —samples of which can be seen in the Plumas County Museum at Quincy.

We climb again, from giant maples and willows along the stream, to oak on the arid slopes, to pine, fir, and incense cedar on the ridges. On entering Lassen Volcanic National Park, we are assured freedom from Positively No Trespassing signs and can wander where we please—or almost where we please.

The park has dangerous thermal areas, hot spots where a thin crust overlies superheated steam chambers or where lakes boil. The Pacific Crest Trail passes the small Terminal Geyser, Boiling Springs Lake (temperature 125 degrees F.), and within 2 miles of the Devils Kitchen, a ravine where steam hisses from small vents.

Odors of hydrogen sulfide in the woods and across the meadows remind us of volcanism once rampant here. Lassen Peak is the Trail's first introduction to the Cascade Range, a series of dramatic volcanoes that extends north through Oregon and Washington into British Columbia. Layers of Cascade lavas now have a depth of as much as 15,000 feet, so surface manifestations only hint at the great bulk of volcanic rock beneath.

These volcanoes, of which Lassen Peak is the southernmost, are relatively recent, geologically speaking. So recent, in fact, that eruptions are still going on. The ejected material is now principally steam, but Lassen Peak exploded in 1917 and could start up again.

A side trip to the summit, over a good trail and fairly easy ascent to 10,457 feet, passes over bare volcanic terrain, lava flows, rock rubble and beneath dacite crags, and from the top one can look down across vast areas of devastation. To the northwest rise the Trinity Alps and Mount Shasta, 80 miles away; to the southwest the Sacramento Valley, in the south the Sierra Nevada, and to the east the Great Basin.

Boiling Springs Lake, Lassen Volcanic National Park

Around Lassen Peak itself lie unmistakable signs of a landscape once flooded with red-hot lava: flows that look as though they had poured out only weeks ago, beds of cinders, and denuded slopes that have barely begun to be revegetated after the searing blasts of sixty years ago.

The most recent eruptions began on May 30, 1914. Lava fragments were expelled from the summit and a new crater formed. Molten material welled up and poured out the following May, and a few days after that came violent explosions that sent clouds of smoke and dust thousands of feet into the air.

Lava pouring down the east side ran into packed snow, resulting in a devastating flow of hot mud, ash, and debris that swept through a mile-wide swath of forest. Three days later, violent explosions hurled clouds of ash high into the air and let out along the ground a superheated blast of gas and ashes that seared everything in its path.

In 1917 the volcanics subsided. Today the National Park Service monitors ground movements in the park because one of the surest signs of pending eruption is an increase in the frequency and magnitude of local earthquakes. That way, there is likely to be advance warning in the future, and people could be evacuated well before any new eruptions begin.

Today the results of this and previous eruptions can be observed on relatively short side trips off the Pacific Crest Trail, which passes through the eastern side of Lassen Volcanic National Park. Good paths lead to Bumpass Hell, a collection of boiling springs and steam vents, to Chaos Crags, the Devastated Area, and numerous lava flows and cinder cones.

Thus we have a dramatic introduction to volcanism in the Cascade Range—a violent series of events that has been transpiring for millions of years. From here to the North Cascades the hiker will be walking much of the time on cinders, lava flows, or soil derived from volcanic sources.

About 40 miles northeast of the Pacific Crest Trail rises the Modoc Plateau, a region of recent volcanics that includes the exceptionally interesting Lava Beds National Monument. Hikers who manage to get there will be well rewarded. Nowhere do we know of a more impressive concentration of explorable lava tunnels, rifts, cones, and lava flows.

North from Lassen Volcanic National Park, one passes scantily vegetated cinder dunes, cones, and lava flows. In between, the route leads through fir and pine forests replete with songs of finches and grosbeaks and chatter of blackbirds.

Regardless of sulfurous fumes here and there, the meadows burst with Queen Anne's lace, and thistles develop into spiny, head-high flowering stalks.

Burney Falls

Eastward lies the Caribou Wilderness; westward is the Thousand Lakes Wilderness. A prominent feature along this part of the trail is Hat Creek Rim, a 20-mile-long fault cliff that rises to 1,500 feet on the east side of Hat Creek. It was lifted during movements along a complex series of interconnected faults, and there are numerous tumbled lava flows at the base, most of them now well vegetated. Within these flows are untold numbers of caves, including Subway Cave, part of a tube that formed when the surface of a lava flow hardened and the inner molten mass moved on. A Forest Service trail leads through part of the cave.

It may seem incongruous to come upon a large waterfall in country so dry and soil so porous. Yet sometimes ground water is effectively channeled through layers of lava underlain by impermeable sedimentary rock. If the rocks should break away in cliffs, the water emerges as springs or falls.

Such is the case at Burney Falls, which plunge 129 feet into a nearly closed amphitheater. The site is preserved in McArthur–Burney Falls Memorial State Park, and an overlook provides visitors with good views of a network of springs whose waters ooze from the rock to make up the falls. The total flow is about 200 million gallons a day.

Ferns and mosses surrounding this amphitheater suggest that the water flows continuously; indeed, it prevails even during times of severe drought in the surrounding region. There must be an immense underground reservoir, because not only does the water issue dependably at all times, it also has a temperature of 42 to 48 degrees summer and winter. The site is not unlike an oasis. Wildlife naturally takes advantage of such a blessing in dry land, and behind the falls is one of the few known nesting sites of the black swift, a swallowlike bird extremely fast in flight.

The park has food, supplies, camp and picnic sites, educational programs, exhibits, and self-guided nature trails. Recreational activities include swimming, fishing, and boating.

Trails through these dense forests toward Mount Shasta are not unlike early trails of the original inhabitants, the Achomawi and Atsugewi Indians. These people did not suffer quite so rapidly the fate of their counterparts in the Sierra Nevada, for here the Gold Rush did not overwhelm them all at once. The effects were similar nonetheless. Multiple use of their terrain deprived them of mammals, salmon, and even land on which to live.

At times the forest through which we pass is a sparse one of ponderosa pines, interspersed with sagebrush, manzanita, and white oak. The unbroken trunks of the pines seem an unusually vivid shade of orange here. At this elevation, 3,000 feet, the summer days can be excruciatingly hot, but the woods are home to deer, porcupines, squirrels, chipmunks, jays, and an abundance of other furred or feathered animals.

We now come upon an unusual plant that hugs the ground in large masses. The last time we saw such matted patches was high in the Sierra Nevada where vegetation often has to hug the rocks as protection against wind, or simply as an adaptation to extremes of hot and cold, wet and dry. This matted plant, totally unlike the alpine species, grows in well-protected areas, and there seems to be no reason for its sprawling growth pattern. One can only explain it as an adaptation and normal manner of growth, and *Ceanothus prostratus* is well named indeed. Its relatives grow to tall shrubs, but this squaw carpet looks like a spreading dwarf holly, replete with interlaced sharp spiny leaves. It produces short-stemmed purplish blue flowers in small clusters.

As the trail turns west, the terrain continues to be relatively unspectacular on long, level lava ridges. Except for Shasta, of course, which we now glimpse through the trees. From ridgetops we get commanding views of it, "its pale, rosy lavas enamelled with ice," as the nineteenth-century geologist, Clarence King, described it.

John Muir avowed that people went to mountains to get their good tidings, but here we find that they go to mountains for more than tidings. They go for pain, misery, mystery, hardship, death, salvation, revelation, and Eternal Life.

In fact, Shasta seems to have had more than the usual occult, legendary, and metaphysical effect on people. A mountain is superhuman, to be sure, at least in the sense that it is larger than human beings, which usually has meant that it must be conquered. But people also regard mountains as "supernatural," and this opens up a new world of fantasy and speculation. Hikers may be particularly susceptible to this free play of ideas and experience because they ramble for a long time with free minds and open hearts. In any case, they are willing to listen and to try to understand.

As they approach Shasta and pass south of it, never nearer than 10 miles, they see it as a colossal white cone—or in late summer, a dark cone spotted with white. It rises to an elevation of 14,162 feet and is mostly treeless. Of stratovolcanic origin, its basaltic and andesitic layers have poured out from the sides or the summit and rolled down the flanks, so that this mountain has some of the longest gentle slopes, pitched at an angle of about 35 degrees, of any volcanic peak.

This has made Shasta tempting to climb because, on certain flanks at least, an ascent requires no special climbing apparatus or technical skills. Clarence King, who climbed the mountain in 1870, wrote in his book *Mountaineering in the Sierra Nevada:* "There is no reason why any one of sound wind and limb should not, after a

Squaw carpet (Ceanothus prostratus)

little mountaineering practice, be able to make the Shasta climb. There is nowhere the shadow of danger and never a real piece of mountain climbing,—climbing, I mean, with hands and feet,—no scaling of walls or labor involving other qualities than simple muscular endurance. . . . Indeed, I have never reached a corresponding altitude with so little labor and difficulty."

The trip does require stamina, however, and the mountain almost seems to challenge human conquest. In fact, this was rather an obsession in the 1920s, when people literally raced to the summit in an effort to beat one another's record. The first ascent is believed to have been in 1854. (Indians may never have gone to the top because they feared and revered the mountain.)

Ordinarily a hiker can make the climb comfortably from tree line to summit, a rise of more than 6,000 feet in a distance of about 3 miles, in six to eight hours. The first record climb established a time of just over four hours, and in subsequent years that was steadily whittled down.

For a long period the record stood at 2 hours, 43 minutes. In 1925 the competitive passion grew so great that a marathon was sponsored and prizes offered. Vigorous, well-trained, record-breaking contestants—athletes in a real sense—signed up, six men in all, plus a lumber-camp boy of eighteen.

You guessed it. It was almost a classic case of *jugend uber alles*. All bets, of course, were on the man who at that time held the unofficial record, and most observers asked only about how much he might better his own time. Meanwhile, the boy made a quick trip to the top and back, the night before the race, just to check out the route and study the condition of the snow.

On the appointed morning, the contestants departed, splitting off on their own favorite routes. The boy, perhaps as expected, made a mistake, took a wrong route, and had to correct his course, thus falling behind and losing precious time.

But those young legs, swinging steadily, soon carried him past all other contestants, and he arrived at the summit in the incredible time of 2 hours and 24 minutes. This amounts to an ascent rate of more than 42 feet per minute, approximately equal to climbing four flights of stairs every minute for nearly 2 hours.

The young man's name was David Lawyer, and he never climbed the mountain again. Nor were any more marathons held. It was an idea whose time came and went, like the old endurance-walking contests of nineteenth-century England when Captain Barclay nearly killed himself by walking a thousand miles in a thousand successive hours.

But beliefs that Shasta holds many mysteries—or solutions to them—still prevail, and probably always will. The early Indians

Castle Crags State Park

thought that the Great Spirit lived there. One also finds the familiar flood legend in Indian stories of Shasta.

Modern beliefs have centered on strange atmospheres, appearing and disappearing images, big people, little people, odd-looking people, flickering lights, giant footprints, and other unusual phenomena.

Occultists think that somewhere inside the mountain live the descendants of the lost continent of Lemuria. Members of the I AM group looked upon Shasta as a place where their founder met Saint Germain.

If the energetic hiker wants to have a try at the summit, it will certainly be a day's work—and then some. According to many who have been there, the best time to start is before dawn, or no later than 4 A.M. It is well to consider certain precautions, and take such survival gear as flashlight, first aid equipment, and food. The terrain is, after all, composed of loose and sometimes jagged volcanic material. Rolling rocks are a real danger, and human lives have been lost from falls or long slides.

Not everyone can go up as John Muir did, rejoicing in the face of a severe blizzard, snuggling down in a snow bank, and remaining not only alive but having all senses alert to the violent wonders of the natural world.

But whoever reaches the top may feel as exhilarated as Clarence King did:

> What volumes of geographical history lay in view! Old mountain uplift; volcanoes built upon the plain of fiery lava; the chill of ice and wearing force of torrent, written in glacier-gorge and water-curved cañon! . . .
> I always feel a strange renewal of life when I come down from one of these climbs; they are with me points of departure more marked and powerful than I can account for upon any reasonable ground. In spite of any scientific labor or presence of fatigue, the lifeless region, with its savage elements of sky, ice and rock, grasps one's nature, and whether he will or no, compels it into a stern, strong accord. Then, as you come again into softer air, and enter the comforting presence of trees, and feel the grass under your feet, one fetter after another seems to unbind from your soul, leaving it free, joyous, grateful!

Shasta is young and still growing. It is the largest volcano in the Cascade Range, covering 17 square miles. The last eruption was probably in 1786, and the next—who can say? In any case, as they pass around it to the south, west, and north, Pacific Crest Trail hikers have it in view for a good many miles.

When they descend into the Sacramento River valley south of Dunsmuir, hikers must be prepared for the roar that never ends:

Interstate Route 5 carries a twenty-four-hour parade of buses, cars and trucks. But if the hikers keep moving, they soon enter Castle Crags State Park and become engulfed once again in a forest of pine, fir, oak, maple, ash, haw, cherry, black cottonwood, and other trees of lower elevations and streamside environments.

Poison oak is also present. In many ravines in these parts, it grows almost in thickets and is tall enough in places for a hiker to brush hands and arms against it unwittingly. Travelers who stay alert and know how to identify the plant should have little trouble.

The tall granite cliffs confronting us signal a diversion. Rather than proceeding due north from Mount Shasta to the next Cascade volcano, the Pacific Crest Trail loops to tour the spectacular Klamath Mountains, referred to by many westerners as the Trinity Alps.

The spectacle begins abruptly and dramatically with Castle Crags. This much-cracked gray granite mass rises in bold relief straight out of dense forest and soars more than 4,000 feet. A short, steep side trail leads among granite buttresses to commanding view-points. The principal ridge lies within Castle Crags State Park, where there are nature trails, campsites, supplies, and rangers on duty.

It is almost the last outpost, or so we feel as we head into the interior of an immense amorphous mass of upended earth. The Klamath Mountains cover some 12,000 square miles, with high ridges and peaks and winding valleys that offer abundant opportunity for wild-country exploration and side trips.

The going can be tough, however, for canyons are deep and rock walls steep. The terrain consists of sedimentary, metamorphic, and volcanic rocks and is covered with dense coniferous forests. This type of terrain dominates the rest of the trail route in California— and on into Oregon until we return to lavas of the Cascade Range.

In some ways we are reminded of the Southern Highlands along the Appalachian Trail in North Carolina and Georgia. The Klamath Mountains are not strung out in a line as is the Sierra Nevada. Here the Pacific Crest Trail winds in and out, following a circuitous route along ridges that carry it from Castle Crags into the Scott, Salmon, Marble, and Siskiyou Mountains. The route does not, however, keep solely to crests; it descends to river crossings and rises again through deep woods. This provides a montage of experiences capped by haze-tinted panoramic views of multiple peaks and ridges. Travelers pass through patches of scrub oak and manzanita and cross glades of bracken fern. The woods seem filled with chipmunks racing about as though a fire were coming.

Sometimes one does. Even a distant fire causes the sky to be blotted out and fills these woods with smoke. At times hikers may make their way through charred fields where the sun beams down and new growth has begun to burgeon.

The sun can be very hot indeed in Klamath country, and when hikers descend to cross a ravine they may feel as though they have entered an oven in which there is little or no circulation of air.

Moreover, in a long, hot summer the air may be dry and the trail dusty, so arriving at streams is refreshing. And it is while drinking that hikers discover some of the most rugged yet delicate beauty of these mountains. Stream boulders seem to be of every conceivable origin—not just volcanic, which has been so familiar from Lassen to Shasta. Here there are almost pure quartz boulders, crystallized concentrations of pyroxene and amphibole, piles of gabbro, granite and schist—some with an almost satiny sheen. All have been polished by constant grinding in steep mountain streams, and together they represent a colorful summary of the geologic origins of the Klamath Mountains.

In addition to designs and colors in boulders, the mountains offer meadows sulfur yellow with composite flowers, red flashing wings of flickers flying from trunk to trunk, and deep maroon of manzanita shrubs.

Now and then we hear the growl of logging trucks and the whine of saws, but this is essentially a wild land.

A hummingbird buzzes by. Three robins rise up to attack an incoming Cooper's hawk. Nuthatches, woodpeckers, finches, siskins. . . . For persons who in the love of nature hold communion, there is more to be done and seen on a single mile of trail in the Klamaths than other hikers might see on a whole day's outing.

This is no place to hurry. With hundreds of discoveries to be made, a traveler may be occupied for hours.

Example: while crossing a meadow to photograph corn lilies one day, we chanced upon a patch of pitcher plants. This was a rare treat even though the plants occur rather widely, and we had seen a botanical reserve set aside for them on the Oregon coast. Conditions must be just right, however, and the plant often grows in remote or hidden moist locations where man does not tread.

We were simply not expecting pitcher plants on this ridgetop meadow. Yet there they were, in soggy spots that could have been the final vestiges of lakes drying up. The life of a lake or pond is limited, anyway, and eventually it fills with organic and inorganic sediment and turns into a bog and perhaps a meadow.

These plants grew in dense clusters and looked almost like a collection of green baseballs from a distance. Each tubular plant was bent over at the top, almost like a miniature green-hooded cobra (the species is sometimts called cobra plant). At the opening were two narrow lobes where nectar, secreted by glands, attracted insects.

Once an insect enters this cylinder, it has little chance of getting out, for nature has fashioned an ingenious deathtrap. The inner walls are covered with overlapping cells equipped with sharp points

Pitcher plants

Peeling bark of madrone tree

extending downward. This makes it virtually impossible for a trapped organism to climb back out. The very presence of foreign objects causes secretions in the bottom of the tube, and it is into this liquid that the visitor finally falls.

Death follows, then decay, then absorption by the plant as a supplement to its food-building processes.

Here is a rare reversal of the customary practice, a system in which plants evolved to eat animals. The walls and hood of the pitcher contain small translucent areas, like so many little windows, possibly designed to attract insects, but also of interest from an esthetic point of view.

The flowers appeared to be entirely separate, rising on long leafless stalks and hanging their dark crimson petals about 8 inches above the pitcher part of the plant.

To budding biologists such wet places, replete with other vegetation and forms of invertebrate animal life, constitute living ecological laboratories. If we could solve one tenth of the mysteries in these little bogs, we might have a keen insight into the mysteries of the universe.

Another natural phenomenon, far more ubiquitous in the low places of these mountains, usurps a hiker's time and is especially attractive to photographers. This is the madrone, a tree with reddish-brown bark of an almost silky finish when young. As the outer bark ages, it cracks and peels into an infinite number of designs, and the peelings make each tree a masterpiece of art and sculpture in its own right. To get enthusiastic about the madrone is to want to photograph them all. Using black-and-white or color film, the results are exceptional, for although the orange outer bark and the green inner bark are colorful, form is the thing here. No palette, no canvas, no sculptor's garden ever had so many variations.

The madrone is a member of the heath family, in the genus *Arbutus,* and characteristic of climates considerably warmer than those tolerated by the familiar firs and pines of the Pacific Crest Trail. The leaves are evergreen, renewed each summer. Flowers, in consonance with the reputation of the heath family (as in the case of azaleas and rhododendrons), are large clusters of creamy-white blossoms that come forth in spring.

While large madrones are rather rare in these mountains, some giant specimens do exist: height, 75 feet; spread, nearly 100 feet; girth, more than 30 feet.

Mostly we see younger and more modest examples standing beside the trail, offering some of the world's greatest works of natural art.

Pinesap, Three Sisters Wilderness

8

The Great Volcanoes

Being now free from anxiety, I was
at leisure to observe minutely the objects
around me.

Francis Parkman, *The Oregon Trail*, 1849

THOUGH PEOPLE TODAY think nuclear explosions enormous and tornadoes destructive, they know nothing equal to what happened at Mount Mazama, site of the present Crater Lake.

A close comparison would be the 1902 eruption of Mont Pelée, on the Caribbean island of Martinique, where searing clouds of red-hot ash and scalding steam blasted across the landscape, killing some 30,000 people.

Here in the Cascades, Mount Mazama exploded more than 6,000 years earlier, and from all the evidence, even Pelée seems small by comparison. Ashes from the Mazama eruptions were blown completely around the world. Between 7 and 9 cubic miles of pumice hurled into the air eventually covered 5,000 square miles of the Oregon countryside to a depth of more than 6 inches.

It is difficult to conceive of so much fire, smoke, steam, lava, and debris flying through the air. But the resultant crater, or caldera, is so huge, 6 miles wide and filled with a lake 1,932 feet deep, that Mazama must surely have been a rival to Shasta. And it boggles the senses to contemplate what would happen in California and around the world if a modern eruption blew off the upper half of Shasta.

Peaceful now, the region once reeked with acrid sulfurous fumes, rocked with earthquakes, lay scorched by lava rivers, and for long periods was darkened by sky-high clouds of smoke and debris.

Crater Lake's rim is a short side trip for the Pacific Crest Trail hiker, but nearly every step one takes to, in, or around the caldera is a step on fallen pumice, congealed lava, or broken rocks. The landscape may be cool now—at 8,000 feet it gets very cold and has an average 50 feet of snow each winter—but in those eruptive days, pumice fell like rain, and layer after layer of lava spewed out, some reaching 35 miles from the source.

Afterward the caldera filled with water, and the amount of moisture entering began to equal that seeping out; hence, the level of the lake fluctuates very little.

The blue of Crater Lake is one of the most vivid in any body of water. It is never quite the same, depending on time of day or state of wind, and at dawn or sunset may not look blue at all. The surface lies nearly 2,000 feet below the highest point on the rim, and the waters are so transparent and mirrorlike that we seem to be looking into a bottomless pit.

Ice also has gripped the land and altered its surface, as glacier-made grooves on the rocks reveal.

Today, notwithstanding the legacy of fire and freezing, the slopes around Crater Lake are clothed with some of the finest mountain hemlock forest in the Pacific Northwest. Cool coves on the mountain flanks, where water oozes from crevices in the lava, have wild gardens of unusual density.

Fir and pine shade them; shrubs of currant and whortleberry advance among them. But competition seems to have no effect on the sphagnum moss, which spills down slopes and forms a soft green bed out of which grow sedge, senecio, paintbrush, bog orchid, and miterwort.

A rainbow of vegetative color enlivens these seeps: bright orange skyrocket gilia, purple Cascade aster, sulfur-yellow buckwheat, magenta fireweed, scarlet Sitka columbine, and lavender monkshood. Sometimes certain species, such as monkey flower, grow in pink and yellow masses. To these places come yellowjackets, butterflies, moths, mammals, birds, and other residents of coniferous woods.

Such abundance does not exist on the pumice desert—an open terrain on the western slope of Mazama's old crater. On that desert the Pacific Crest Trail hiker breaks out of pine forest and heads across a sand-colored sea of pumice, scoria, and ash, and may seem to have entered some detached section of Death Valley. For, in the more than six thousand years since this pumice was superheated and blown here at speeds of 100 miles an hour, the sterile ground has been receptive to few plants.

Slowly, however, organic soil has begun to accumulate, and the pioneers—pussy-paws, knotweeds, lodgepole pines—are gaining rootholds.

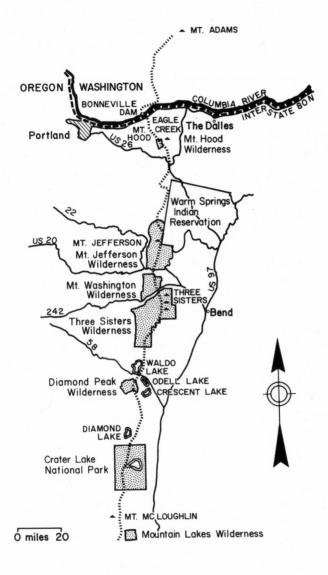

THE PACIFIC CREST TRAIL IN OREGON

All these contrasts are not limited to the Crater Lake area. Indeed, from the California border north into Oregon and on to Crater Lake National Park, the hiker passes through arid and humid, hot and cold environments. In open stands of ponderosa pines, at elevations below 4,000 feet, heat waves rise and the ground dries out. Grass turns brown. The large-leaved mule-ears shrivels in early summer. Sharp-spined thistles and squaw carpet grow in open and sunny places. Lizards scurry over logs. Few birds but chickadees move about in the hot hours.

Anxious for shade, we come to a section where mile after mile is composed of sawn stumps, slashed trees, and downed logs.

Veering east of the Siskiyou Mountains, the trail winds back and forth, keeping a steady course to the north. Ahead looms remarkably symmetrical Brown Mountain and beyond that the high cone of Mount McLoughlin. Surrounded by volcanoes in various stages of erosional disintegration, the trail arrives at Lake of the Woods.

From here, a side trip 5 miles to the east leads into the Mountain Lakes Wilderness, 23,071 acres of rolling, lake-studded upland covered by forests interspersed with meadows.

Continuing north, we rise slowly in elevation. The surroundings begin to take on a more humid aspect, and a forest of firs and mountain hemlocks closes in. The open spaces characteristic of ponderosa pine forest are here filled with wild rose, currant, and dozens of other types of shrubs. Huckleberries dangle their fruits—and time after time we stop to sample them.

Except for occasional meadows edged by tree trunks that look like Roman columns, the forest assumes complete command and blots out the far horizon. Our attention in such locales focuses not on distant panoramas but on things beside or above the trail. Pipsissewa and pyrola, for example. These small pink-flowered plants inhabit places of deepest shade and can easily be overlooked. Even when we find them, we must examine their form and structure closely to appreciate them. Both in the shinleaf family, they hang their flowers downward like bells. The pipsissewa is called wintergreen because its leaves stay green year round, not because of the fragrance more associated with *Gaultheria,* in the heath family. Both species give the plant community a pastel rose-pink coloration complementary to the multiple greens of moss and fern.

Shiny leaves of twinflower glisten like metal in the sunshine. In places, fallen logs make the going difficult. A sugar pine now and then reminds us of the mountains of California; but we shall soon see the last of this species with its immense cones.

For a while we seem to encounter fewer clear-cut areas, but alas, we come to the tracks of a bulldozer that crashed through the forest years ago, tearing up trees and leaving deep ruts.

Beargrass (lily family)

North of Crater Lake the forest is lodgepole pine for miles around. The trees grow so closely together that the weaker are pruned and dying, leaning on their healthier neighbors. All seem the same size and age, suggesting a sweep of wildfire years ago. Some grow in twisted form, owing probably to the weight of winter snow.

The naked trunks, whether standing or fallen crisscrossed on the forest floor, often exhibit complex engravings made by insects that once burrowed under the bark.

Pinesap, a saprophytic member of the heath family, here and there grows from decaying logs. Reddish stems and brown and yellow fruit are unique and notable among these trailside plants.

In other places the lodgepole forest has a cleaner floor, littered only with needles and having an occasional lupine or dwarf manzanita.

We do not tarry in any one place, however, because large black flies are persistent along this stretch. It almost seems that where the forest is at its most beautiful, the flying invertebrates are at their most abundant. The Pacific Crest Trail hiker comes to accept that, or else does not find the experience as joyful as expected. One learns to take the trail environment as is.

Soon the environment changes sharply from open woods of lodgepole pine to a near rain forest, where firs and hemlocks predominate and the plants about our feet include fireweed, bog orchid, and dwarf dogwood. We can tell that we are getting farther north because of the increasing abundance of beargrass, that tall-stalked lily with a waving, cream-colored head of densely clustered flowers.

Here in central Oregon the lakes become more numerous and we pass some large ones: Diamond, Crescent, Summit, Odell, and Waldo.

We also pass trail junction after trail junction, which reminds us that the Pacific Crest Trail is part of a complex system of hiking routes. Almost steadily throughout Oregon we go through national forests, each of which has many miles of well-mapped paths. These reach fascinating destinations, such as wild and beautiful swimming sites, botanical reserves, geological points of interest, caves, falls, springs, and lakes, many accessible only by trail.

These off-the-beaten paths also reach secluded fishing spots and give access to campgrounds where hikers can relax on layover days, establish a base of operations, and resupply if a store is handy.

There is almost no limit to the exploration potentials of these thousands of miles of side trails. Finding and following them is usually very simple. Guidebooks to the Pacific Crest Trail denote and describe all major junction points. Colorful maps of each national park and forest are available at ranger stations, supervisors' headquarters, regional offices, and in Washington, D.C.

United States Geological Survey topographic maps may be purchased at local outlets as well as at Survey map offices listed in Appendix 3, though these topographic maps do not show the Pacific Crest Trail. National Forest maps indicate the route officially as Trail #2000.

For detailed guidance to major trails in the northwestern states, including some not associated with the Pacific Crest Trail, descriptive books are available, including such titles as *Wilderness Trails Northwest, 100 Oregon Hiking Trails,* and *Short Trips and Trails: The Columbia Gorge.* These and other guidebooks are listed in the Bibliography.

Between Crescent and Odell Lakes the Pacific Crest Trail curves westward along Whitefish and Trapper Creeks through the 35,440-acre Diamond Peak Wilderness. Named for John Diamond, who climbed the peak in 1852, this area consists of dense forest, lakes, and open volcanic slopes. Modern hikers can climb to the 8,744-foot summit with relative ease—unless snow is too much of a problem. Given good fortune and the right conditions, they may see deer, elk, bear, and smaller mammals, water ouzels along streams, and buffleheads and golden-eyes on the dozens of small lakes.

By the time we reach the Three Sisters Wilderness, the volcanic nature of the landscape becomes more obvious than ever. Indeed, there has been more volcanic activity in this region during the past few thousand years than in any other part of the Cascade Range.

Even back at Trapper Creek the boulders in the stream were almost entirely basalt. Now we come to extraordinary collections of lava peaks, crags, craters, flows, obsidian cliffs, cinder cones, and forbidding terrain where forms and designs challenge the imagination.

The Pacific Crest Trail hiker need not adopt a moonwalker's suit to get across this rugged domain, though there are places where it would certainly be inadvisable to go barefoot.

One walks on glass, literally, in places where obsidian outcrops or has been concentrated by erosion. Usually the small fragments of this quartz-based rock offer no problem, but their broken edges can be sharp, a feature the early Indians utilized in making obsidian projectile points.

In all likelihood, black dust will infiltrate one's eyes, ears, nose, clothes, and equipment during a sojourn in or through the area. But those are minor matters compared with the grandeur of nature's productions here.

The Pacific Crest Trail passes along the western slopes of the Three Sisters—South, Middle, and North—all of which rise to more than 10,000 feet. They are the results of both quiet and violent volcanism; some of the outpourings must have been spectacular. Glaciation gripped the peaks afterward and reworked their profiles; glaciers, glacial valleys, and moraines can readily be seen today. Collier Glacier, on the North Sister, is the largest in Oregon.

The different types of terrain—gentle and precipitous, reliable and unreliable, safe and dangerous—make the climbing of these peaks a task to be undertaken with prudence and proper preparations. The summits can be gained with varying degrees of difficulty, but the routes need to be carefully selected.

From the top, one sees that these three peaks lie in the center of a string of volcanoes from Mount McLoughlin on the south to Mount Hood on the north.

Even though there is a great deal of more or less barren lava in the Three Sisters Wilderness, the 48-mile stretch of Pacific Crest Trail in it goes mostly through forest or across meadows and threads among large numbers of shallow lakes and ponds. The volcanic soil, powdery and soft in spots—almost like black flour—supports buckwheat, pussy-paws, penstemon, paintbrush, lupine, and other plants that can get along in dry environments.

There is no dearth of butterflies to circulate from flower to flower, or chickadees, juncos, and nuthatches to chatter in the hemlocks.

We often admire the arrangements of hemlock cones on the ground, and the way lodgepole pine cones collect in masses. These have been laid out in haphazard fashion, obviously, but they also seem to have a peculiar design and cohesion. Mostly they lie in shade, but when early morning sun spotlights them, or they are touched by a golden stream of sunset color, there is nothing routine or commonplace about them. The trailside has more art than a thousand museums.

Coming to open meadows, we get good views of the Sisters, and pass small depressions recently filled with water but now abounding in thick growths of grass and sedge.

Once, while watching the scene reflected in a shallow lake, we heard the clatter of horses' hooves, and in a moment saw a group of riders race in a splashing gallop across the far end of the shallow waters. Such illegal acts have polluted more than one lake in the Three Sisters Wilderness and elsewhere along the trail, and given force to the arguments of those who would eliminate domestic animals from wilderness areas or sharply control the behavior of wilderness users.

Dry, hot, dusted with lava powder, we drop into a forested ravine and kneel beside a spring. The pure waters issue forth at 42 degrees. Nothing could be more welcome—and no waters were ever more delicious. This near-icy water in the midst of summer is testimony to the insulative properties of lava.

In this habitat, we find pinesap growing in front of a beetle-engraved log and photograph it so that the transitory form and design will not be lost. We come to an upturned root with twisted

Mountain hemlock cones

grain and make a picture of that. Then a patch of fallen cones—and another picture.

Were we to photograph each splendid sight along the trail, we might never depart the Three Sisters Wilderness.

So we resolve to quit making photographs (at least for a while) and go on to McKenzie Pass. But then we come to a bizarre and picturesque no-man's land as we enter the Mount Washington Wilderness. And the camera comes out again. Hikers should take along ample supplies of film if they wish to record their travels adequately.

This is not the first time we have walked over raw and rugged lava, so jagged that it seems to have been ejected from the earth only yesterday. (The age of the youngest flow has been estimated at 2,700 years, truly young by geologic standards.)

But though the trail is well constructed and walkers do not endanger their shins, the immense sweep of landscape left by the Yapoah and associated lava flows appears like something out of delirium tremens.

The broken, black terrain has upheaval ridges, lava gutters, cooling cracks, and cinder fields, and we seem to be adrift in a lifeless sea of basalt. Yet lichens have begun to spread. Six species of conifers grow, though still small trees, like advance scouts from forests beyond. Marmots inhabit the crevices, birds nest in the conifers, and toads and spiders may be seen.

Passing over lava flows east of Belknap Crater, the Pacific Crest Trail proceeds through the Mount Washington Wilderness and shortly afterwards enters the Mount Jefferson Wilderness.

Provisions of the Wilderness Act of 1964, plus regulations of the U.S. Forest Service, make it clear that these special lands are to be handled tenderly and pertinent sections of the Code of Federal Regulations are prominently posted: "Occupancy restrictions. Under the authority of the Secretary of Agriculture . . . and in order to promote, perpetuate, and restore the wilderness character of the land, the following acts are prohibited: Bringing or having any pack or saddle animal within a distance of 200 feet from the shore line of any lake within the Mount Jefferson Wilderness, Three Sisters Wilderness, Mount Washington Wilderness, and Diamond Peak Wilderness, except for the purpose of watering, loading, unloading or travel through on established routes. Violators are subject to prosecution."

Motorized vehicles and equipment are also prohibited at all times.

It is a relief, indeed, that in these quiet woods we do not have to anticipate the roar of motors. We walk in cathedrallike woods of hemlock and fir, festooned by black and green lichens strung out along the limbs.

Going around Mount Jefferson, the Pacific Crest Trail keeps to the west, through heavily forested parts of the wilderness. Between

Upturned root, Three Sisters Wilderness

these dense woods and the vegetation on the other side of Mount Jefferson is a pronounced contrast. On the dry eastern slopes only some 15 to 20 inches of rain fall annually, while here the precipitation, including snow, amounts to ten times as much.

The forest is often broken by lakes, stream courses, places where avalanches or rockslides may have swept through in the past, and open ridges where elevation and climatic conditions are not conducive to growth.

The trail swings around the flank of Three Fingered Jack, a volcano in which the internal structure is unusually well preserved, across milky creeks laden with light-colored silt of glacial origin, and over exposed ridges from which one gets close views (in fact, too close) of 10,497-foot Mount Jefferson.

Ironically, the views of the peak from up here are not overwhelming. Better to stop on the approach routes and appreciate the mountain as it rises in a deep blue sky, a scene framed in summer by rose-red rhododendrons. Or look back as we proceed north and take in the panorama with Jefferson Park, a lake-studded vale, in the foreground.

The botanical resources of the west side of Mount Jefferson are so immense and attractive they can scarcely be comprehended in a short visit. But as we travel northward, this is a good introduction to the abundant vegetation of the North Cascades.

Whatever the combination of soil and climate, nature somehow endows individual plants here with some of the richest color we have ever seen. The paintbrush, for example. Close up, it resembles an exploding rocket on the night of the Fourth of July, a scarlet so vivid it makes the flower seem to glow with a kind of volcanic inner fire.

The penstemon, similarly, bursts out with such an unusual blue and purple that one wonders whether some special ingredient in the soils of Mount Jefferson accounts for it. Perhaps we merely get carried away by the contrast of sunlit flowers against dark volcanic rock.

In any case, the hiker passes a succession of species: bleeding heart in shady places; sprays of rhododendron hanging over the trail; dense yellow flower clusters of mountain ash along open stream courses. Maple thickets are alive with warblers. Near the splashing spray of hurtling floodwaters grow both pink and yellow monkey flowers.

Deeper within the woods, the aspect is far from shadowy. Sunlight sifts down among the hemlocks and strikes the multiple leaves of vine maple. White light is converted to green, and each leaf becomes a beacon that transfers this new color to the surroundings.

Through filtered green, therefore, we hike from vale to vale, a sharp contrast to the barren lavas above.

Trees have fallen across each other and lie rotting, the jumbled

Mount Jefferson

Vine maple, Mount Jefferson Wilderness

mass covered with lichens, moss, hemlock needles, and ankle-high flowering bunchberry. However, not all is soft and harmless. The vicious spines of devil's club lie sequestered in moister places.

The duff of centuries has collected in these woods. Foliose lichens cling to the trunks of trees. Logs that fell across streams created waterfalls. Strands of boulders in these streams have become almost entirely covered with sphagnum moss and lie interspersed with trilliums and wood violets.

A rush of air blows out of these roaring watery channels and cools the brow of the weary hiker.

Above the seething stream, chaff, insects, spiders, and spider webs float through the air. It may be calm along the trail, but sometimes the trees shake in gusts of gale force that race through their tops. And more than once we see trees scarred and charred by lightning.

For the most part, however, this wood remains quiet in summer, undisturbed by the elements. Except perhaps for snow: In the middle of July one year we stopped at a ranger station to inquire about access to the Pacific Crest Trail just north of Mount Jefferson.

"No use trying," came the reply, emphasized by a shake of the head. "Parts of it are buried under forty-seven feet of snow."

East of Olallie Butte and the Mount Jefferson Wilderness lies the Warm Springs Indian Reservation, and we are reminded that these woods, streams, and lakes were first known and utilized by northwestern Indians.

The Pacific Crest Trail passes west of Olallie Butte, and so the hiker may not meet the residents of the Reservation. But this could be done at Kahneeta, where the Indians have developed a recreation resort with hot mineral pools, accommodations, camping, and fishing. The resort is not all that makes the Warm Springs Reservation a lively place, for there are fishing, boating, and swimming on reservoirs behind Pelton and Round Butte dams.

Such efforts are encouraged by the federal government, a situation far different from that which the ancestors of these Indians suffered in the Pacific Northwest. There were dozens of tribes in the region before the white man arrived, and the journals of Lewis and Clark contain the first written descriptions of Chinooks, Spokanes, Yakimas, Killamucks, and Klickitats, among others.

For a while, the traders, trappers, and settlers who arrived after Lewis and Clark got along fairly well with the inhabitants. But then the Indians began to die off from epidemics of diseases brought in by the newcomers, and some tribes were nearly wiped out.

So many whites poured into the Northwest that the visits became an invasion, alarming the Indians. Worse yet, settlers cleared lands that belonged to the Indians, and that led to attacks and counterattacks, battles, massacres, and wars from the 1840s to 1880.

The pattern resembled that infamous reduction of aboriginal tribes in the Sierra Nevada and southern California, a pattern that included even the influx of miners seeking gold. In 1857 miners and prospectors poured into Washington and British Columbia, battling with the Indians over lands assigned to the tribes.

The whole unhappy history played itself out again: decimation of tribes, establishment and alteration of treaties, removal of Indians to reservations.

Today some 3,600 Indians live in Oregon's two reservations, the Umatilla and Warm Springs, which together occupy more than 650,000 acres. The latter area is home to members of the Warm Springs, Wasco, and certain Northern Paiute tribes. In addition to commercial recreation activities, the people of the reservation are involved in lumbering and other enterprises.

We look back south and get a view of Mount Jefferson's snowy mass either standing aloft in a dark blue sky, or wreathed with clouds.

From here north such open views become rare as we walk more and more in relatively undisturbed forest. For miles we seem to be the only human beings to have come this way since the early Indians. That is simply our imagination, except that we now begin to hike through more remote regions and away from such popular spots as Mount Jefferson. Here the Pacific Crest Trail *is* a bit less traveled.

The forest is not all undisturbed, however. We are soon jarred into reality by entering an area clear-cut for logging purposes. If the site is scenically altered, at least the open sunlight is good for ceanothus and beargrass, which grow so thickly that they somewhat resemble snow spilling down the slope.

The beargrass looks like grass, in a way, because the leaves are elongate. But grasses don't have flowering stalks like these. The plant is a lily, which sends up a densely flowering head that at first is almost globular in shape, but continues to grow and stretch out in various shapes up to 15 inches long. The stalk itself may eventually rise to 6 feet.

The hiker finds beargrass on relatively dry and open slopes, but it also grows in forests and shady places up to 6,000 feet elevation. The plant is part of nature's scheme to heal the scars of burns and cuts, although even nature requires quite a while to fill denuded areas. Lupines spring up. Maples spread. Rhododendrons venture out. And after hundreds of years the forest would, if undisturbed, restore itself.

We return to the woods for steady progress north, with only tantalizing glimpses of a great white mountain ahead.

The forest floor is a pad of duff, soil, vegetation, and hemlock cones. A canopy closes out the light, yet giant Douglas firs grow here, some of them 20 feet in circumference. Rays of sunlight coming in obliquely illuminate the furrowed bark, which is covered with mosses, lichens and, in the crevices, layer after layer of cobwebs.

The more we travel, the more we appreciate nature's simple and flexible laws. The amount of light that manages to get through the canopy determines what plants grow where; if a little more than usual descends we have anemone, trillium, and vanilla leaf in richer display.

But when we break out into a meadow bursting with sunlight, the change is striking. Everything tries to grow at once, the species crowding on one another. Grasses spring up interspersed with lupine, bluebells, clover, violet, buttercup, rose, thistle, parsley, paintbrush. . . . Even a tiny depression devoid of vegetation is filled with spider webs coated with droplets of moisture.

A marsh wren flies from one corn lily to another, and our ears are filled with the music of a stream threading its way across the meadow.

The next moment we enter a densely wooded grove, and are again dominated by Douglas fir. Ever since the southern Sierra Nevada, we have been more or less dominated by that tree, and should by now be aware that few conifers are as widespread as the Douglas fir in the mountain West. It is distributed from Mexico to Canada, and to the timber industry is more valuable than any other tree. Twenty-four percent of all trees cut for commercial purposes in the United States are Douglas fir.

It is not a true fir; its cones can be distinguished from others by the three-pointed bracts that present a somewhat spiny appearance. Douglas fir avoids high summits; hikers encounter it on lower slopes and in secluded vales that rest more or less in ecological repose. Under optimum conditions, these giants may live more than a thousand years and attain a height of over 300 feet. They reach their maximum growth in western Oregon and Washington.

Suddenly we break out of the forest and there is Mount Hood, a ponderous pinnacle of snow and lava, utterly massive and overwhelming because it rises above all else, disconnected and unattached, held down by its roots alone.

The summits of these volcanoes of the central Cascades, distinguished by their grand isolation and regal preeminence, lead into what sometimes seem forbidding, hostile regions of the upper atmosphere, mysterious but attainable. From certain high points we can see them all: Jefferson, Hood, Adams, St. Helens—and the highest, Rainier.

The Pacific Crest Trail goes up toward the western shoulder of Mount Hood, and we are eager to climb. But a more earthly phenomenon delays us: huckleberries. Open burnt-over ridges in Mount Hood National Forest produce literally thousands of gallons of berries each season, and picking these is one of the principal public pastimes in late July and early August.

Wild blackberries rank second. Then there are raspberries. Not many people pick elderberries, though it is beginning to be discovered that these make good wine.

We come to another open view of Mount Hood, but now it is draped with clouds that drift over the summit on a high wind. We get only glimpses of the topmost crags, and while this may vex us, there is also a sense of expectancy that each new opening in the clouds will reveal something different. The mountain is the same, of course, but cloud patterns are always changing, a scene sometimes more dramatic than white mountains in clear sky.

Tree line on Mount Hood is fairly low—about 6,000 feet—and as we climb, we find more scarce the sheltered places where massive trunks of Douglas firs branch out in an interlocking network of limbs and needles.

Slowly we leave this behind. Very slowly, if there is much snow on the trail. One year we encountered 10 feet of snow in the trail on the Fourth of July at 4,000 feet. Characteristically, the snow in the trail is peaked like a house roof and a hiker slides off on one side or the other.

But that was a year of exceptionally heavy snow and cool spring weather. Normally in midsummer the hiker can proceed without problems and rise above the forest.

Before getting out of the woods entirely we come to Barlow Pass, historically significant because it was the first road built over the Cascade Range. It was also a branch of the Oregon Trail. Why the pioneers went to all the trouble of building a road over the mountains when the Columbia River had cut a perfect pass through them seems incomprehensible at first. All the newcomers had to do was simply float down the Columbia, turn south, and proceed overland toward the promised lands of the Willamette Valley.

But it was not that simple, largely because falls, rapids, and currents in the river could be extremely hazardous. So instead of taking a chance on losing all their possessions—and themselves—beneath the waters, the emigrants preferred a safer, more predictable route, however difficult to negotiate.

In 1845–46 Samuel K. Barlow, from Kentucky, constructed the first road, a rugged path across this southern flank of Mount Hood. It followed an old Indian trail and was by no means easy to negotiate with horses and wagons; it was also closed by snow much of the year. Yet the newcomers still preferred it to braving the perils of the Columbia River.

Even in late July we find spring flowers coming up through melting snow, the leaves of shrubs opening, and the fiddlenecks of ferns uncoiling.

Above that the vegetation grows smaller and scantier, and by the time we have passed Timberline Lodge we feel once again almost on top of the world.

The summit of Mount Hood, however, is at 11,235 feet, and the Pacific Crest Trail goes no nearer than 3 miles. Naturally it is tempting to take off on a side excursion and climb to the top. But the climb is something more than an excursion. True, it is not terribly difficult, which makes it a popular trek; the Forest Service thinks it may be the most frequently climbed snow-capped peak this side of Fujiyama. Still, it is classed as a technical climb, and even when the snow is least—in late summer—the Service recommends that inexperienced climbers hire a guide and rent proper equipment.

Mount Hood was volcanically active in the 1800s and still emits steam and other gases. At sunset it can turn to a fiery orange or purple or gold from the peaceful rays of a sinking sun. The rocks, the snow, the air, even the clouds take on a uniform hue, as though all light were filtered through a slice of amber.

The world of human occupancy and industry lies below, under or beyond the trees, sometimes beneath a frightful pall of smoke. At times we seem almost stranded on an island. We can breathe and see for miles and rejoice in the original earth. But we are also as though on an ark, adrift on a flood of smog that drowns all else.

This symbolic feeling does not last very long, but the more we hike on the Pacific Crest Trail the more we feel like refugees who cling to the last vestiges of natural beauty, clean air, and serenity.

From the open upper ridges of Mount Hood we descend to some of the most cloistered sections and lowest elevations along the Pacific Crest Trail.

For a short distance the route switchbacks through a corner of the Mount Hood Wilderness, which protects the northern and western summit area, and then zigzags down into forest, past clear-cuts and eventually to the Columbia River Gorge.

If we don't mind a popular trail and a considerable number of hikers, we can divert from the Pacific Crest Trail and go down the Eagle Creek Trail, one of the most delightful approaches to the Columbia River.

The creek is replete with waterfalls, high bluffs, and hair-raising cliffs around which the hiker can progress by clinging to a cable if he has acrophobia.

The Eagle Creek route is lined with luxuriant vegetation, including ferns, sphagnum moss, and many species of flowers that have become dominant since we passed Mount Jefferson. All life forms

Columbia River Gorge

seem abundant, some of them unfamiliar; we observe a spider with yellow body, green legs, and maroon markings.

Kingfishers and swallows fly up and down the stream. Wrens' and warblers' songs are heard above the roar of waterfalls. And there are waxwings, grosbeaks, thrushes, ouzels, hummingbirds. Eagle Creek is unquestionably a biological paradise; the Forest Service maintains 52,000 acres around it in roadless status.

The route of the Pacific Crest Trail itself into the Columbia River Gorge brings a traveler down along talus slopes, first with forest, then without, from which one obtains panoramas of brown lava cliffs, dense woods, deep side canyons and leaping streams.

Western tanagers fly out from the edges of cliffs, their songs lost rapidly to the roar of creeks below. We are accompanied partway by a chickadee flitting from shrub to shrub.

Down near the bottom, the trail is enclosed by maples one moment and Douglas fir the next. Then we cross an open slope with loosened rocks and must tread carefully.

Eventually we round a bend and come to the end of the Oregon Skyline Trail by descending into a roar of interstate highway traffic, aircraft, and locomotives.

We have come to the Columbia, largest river on the Pacific Crest Trail, and in fact the largest North American river emptying into the Pacific Ocean. The trail crosses the Bridge of the Gods, beneath which the water flows at a rate of 88 million gallons a minute. It is hardly free-flowing, however. It originates some 1,100 miles upstream and in getting this far passes more than 170 dams of at least 5,000-acre-feet capacity.

This is the lowest point on the Pacific Crest Trail, approximately 100 feet elevation. Though we are still 145 miles upstream from the Pacific Ocean, this actually marks the beginning of the tide line. Just downstream is Bonneville Dam, the first power dam on the river.

At midstream we enter the state of Washington, and on the north side, after a short circuit upstream, start climbing out of the gorge —midst poison oak, rattlesnakes, and all.

Deception Falls

9

North Cascades

The rivers are our brothers.

Chief Seattle, 1854

EVEN THOUGH VEGETATION hangs over the trail and may get us sopping wet with dew, we can hardly complain in the face of what Lewis and Clark and their colleagues had to endure in the early 1800s. At least, with foresight, we needn't suffer uncertainty of food as they did, or worry about encountering hostile Indians who could end our expedition on the spot.

Indeed, we are able in these modern excursions to enjoy the best of both worlds: to see the scenery somewhat as they did, to have a wilderness experience partly like theirs, and to enjoy the benefits of modern technology that has reduced the weight of food and equipment so that we can carry a week's supply on our backs.

Coming out of the Columbia River Gorge, we have a broad panorama of Mount St. Helens to the west, Mount Rainier to the north, and Mount Adams to the northeast. Behind us, the still dramatic bulk of Mount Hood rises.

All are more or less protected within national forests or parks, a rather heartening portent for the future. On and around these prominent peaks human beings have proved that they can call a halt to the irrational spread of industry, housing, and agriculture and say, "Let this alone."

We had grown accustomed to luxuriant vegetation on the southern side of the river and for a while forgot about life of semiarid regions. But the screech of a Steller's jay brings it back again, and the reappearance of oaks, ponderosa pines, penstemons, and yarrows is confirmation. Maple and hazel line the path. Douglas fir rises high

181

overhead. And the ubiquitous poison oak, sometimes hip high, closes in upon us. Soon, however, we leave all this behind.

The trail proceeds steadily north, and we return to shady vales, rain forests, and berry fields. Logging roads seem to become more numerous, but are offset by blue-green lakes and rippling creeks. We pass an old Indian racetrack, just one of so many interesting features on this or side trails that we could not see them all if we had the whole summer at our disposal.

Mount Adams looms larger through the trees. Glaciers on it remind us that this is snow country and the approaches to the mountain, including low areas, can be deeply covered with snow even in mid-July. Hence travel here is partly dependent on the vagaries of weather.

Once the snow relaxes its grip, there is seldom a dull moment in these woods, especially if the observer forgets to apply insect repellent.

We encounter mountain streams cascading through fern patches and clumps of huge-leaved skunk cabbage. Crossing on crude log bridges (where there are any bridges at all), we pass trilliums, roses, and wood violets, stopping to marvel at the designs of shelf fungus growing on downed logs. If we are hungry, and the season is right, we wade into berry thickets.

Elongate mounds of earth cross the forest floor, once probably under-snow runways of small mammals. Beargrass grows exuberantly in sunny places, and we are now and then startled by bright blue combinations of penstemons and lupines.

The forest is redolent with scents of pine and moldering duff.

Though manipulated by human beings, that is, severely cut years ago, the forest is slowly growing back. This suggests that the preservation of devastated areas is not altogether useless; rather, in moist climates these sites grow over with dense vegetation in nature's persistent succession of species. Thus new wilderness areas can sometimes be established on lands disturbed by human activities.

Winding through wild gardens and deep woods, the trail enters the Mount Adams Wilderness, containing 32,400 acres. The mountain itself, at 12,326 feet the second highest in Washington, is composed of ash and cinders, basaltic and andesitic lava flows, and rounded domes enveloped in ice.

The Pacific Crest Trail takes hikers across the western shoulder of the mountain, and hence they do not see at close hand the largest glacier, which is on the opposite side. However, soon after passing the wilderness boundary, one encounters a Round-the-Mountain Trail, which provides an opportunity to see this glacier and to get to know the mountain better.

As for climbing the summit, there is little problem in summer, although one should choose the route with care and check on snow and weather conditions before making the attempt.

The trail emerges onto open terrain and proceeds beneath glaciers, where travelers have to leap across plunging, silt-laden milky creeks. From certain vantage points one can gain superb views of the scenery ahead, principally Mount Rainier and the Goat Rocks.

Adams itself, in our opinion, is most impressive at sunset, especially when viewed from at least a mile away, with the silhouetted forest providing a foreground. The brilliant white snow of daytime takes on pastel colors as clouds on the western horizon filter the rays of the sun. Dazzling white turns first to gentle yellow. The crags that show through snow and ice change from lava brown to amethyst purple or garnet. A mist develops out of nowhere, forming a cap over the western brow of the peak and enclosing the summit in a soft cottony envelope. This looks stationary, as though nothing were happening, but a banner of mist now and then leaps up from the rest, hurled high by summit breezes, and subsequently folds under again.

Shifting cloud banks on the horizon obscure, then reveal, the sun, projecting onto the mountain a continuous display of shadows and designs.

In July, sunset lasts from seven to nine P.M., time enough for casual changes in colors and patterns. When the birds settle down, the silence of the woods becomes almost supreme.

The cloud cap filters the final, faintly purple rays of the sun, darkening the ravines and turning the lavas from garnet to black. The level of illumination sinks, and night takes over. But the mountain never wholly disappears, remaining as a formless ghostly presence among the stars.

Were the moon to rise, and the cloud cap disappear, and a chorus of coyotes fill the night air, we would not get to sleep for a long time.

Eventually, our eyes, having observed a thousand sights today, can endure no more. The mountain splits into multiple images and dissolves in the veil of sleep.

From Mount Adams north, the Pacific Crest Trail follows the western boundary of the Yakima Indian Reservation, one of 22 such areas that total more than 1.8 million acres in the state of Washington. At present, the Secretary of the Interior has trust responsibility over the reservations, and his department participates in service and development programs until such time as the trust is terminated.

Next, the Pacific Crest Trail winds for 35 miles around ridges, across headwaters, beside glaciers and through high forests of the Goat Rocks Wilderness. Like mountain goats for which the reserve was named, hikers climb to high crags from which they get stunning views not only of the snow-dappled ridges close by but of Mounts Adams, St. Helens, and Rainier. These mountains shine with a bril-

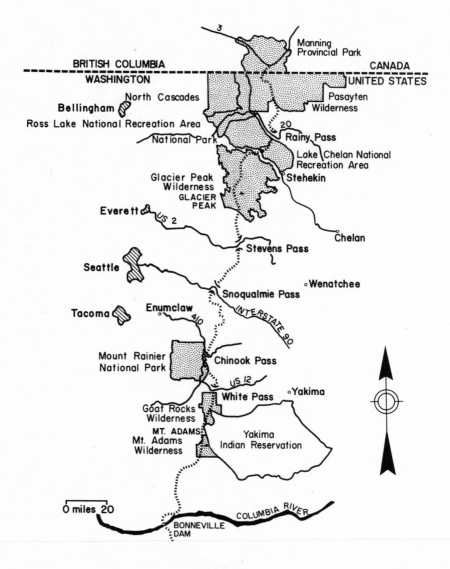

THE PACIFIC CREST TRAIL IN WASHINGTON

liant clear white in the morning but a translucent glacier blue in the afternoon as they become tempered by haze.

The snow may be pleasant to watch from afar, but some people begin to object when it gets underfoot. And the walker in these high regions can very well expect to encounter it through mid-August, if not even into September. The alpine environment, endowed with massive infusions of moist air from the Pacific Ocean, consists of snowfields, frozen lakes, ice masses, and glaciers, frequently laved by an icy wind. Scant wonder that trees grow little more than a foot high.

The trail can be rough and slippery, hazardous enough to make snow gear desirable in the early part of summer. But the effort is worthwhile when it enables us to look into spectacular canyons several thousand feet deep, such as those made by Walupt Creek, Klickitat River, and Upper Lake Creek.

By the time we make our way along these windblown ridges, and zigzag down into White Pass, we feel exhilarated, exuberant, exhausted. And we find it amusing to watch tourists being lifted up the mountain on a chair lift.

It is Sunday, and we have trouble crossing U.S. Route 12 because of a steady stream of camper vehicles descending to Yakima Valley. We observe this with pleasure, though, for these wanderers, in their enthusiasm for the outdoors, help keep recreation areas alive. Impatient hikers may deplore having to cross busy highways, but those vehicles indicate a national interest that nourishes the political energy necessary to keep trails and wilderness areas protected.

The path becomes clogged with snow, but we go on nonetheless. The snow is deeper in the trail, mounded as we have seen before. Alongside, trees rise from melted "wells," so that we move in a somewhat surrealistic world of pits.

In this time of summer melting, the forest is by no means silent. Wind sighs through and moves one tree against another, combining in a double concerto the high violins of needles and the lower cellos of limbs. Thrushes sing and jays send shrieks and chatters. The streams make their music, though partly muffled by bridges of snow.

As a matter of fact, there is much to be said for hiking in snow. It is not all that difficult unless one is on dangerous slopes, where nylon ropes, crampons, and other professional paraphernalia are essential.

In forests, however, the going is easier. Getting lost can be a problem if markers or blazes are not visible. But otherwise there are grand rewards and minor miracles: natural bridges of snow, fresh waterfalls, and marsh marigolds that push up through 4 inches of snow to bloom. So many discoveries await that we shall not get very far. Then, too, we may fall through a snow bridge into a soggy marsh. Getting wet is part of the game on this trail. Even after the snow is gone, water often runs down the path, so the hiker must find a route beside rather than in the trail.

Before highways smoothed out passage across the countryside and bridges made river crossings easy, pioneers generally took the path of least resistance. This didn't mean much at first because the terrain offered so much resistance. But diligent search revealed the principal passes offering access to the west.

In the North Cascades we come to a string of well-known passes, starting with White Pass. Trees keep us from observing how steep the sides of these passes are, so it is difficult to imagine the rough and circuitous original routes and the tough job people had getting their wagons over. Even going downhill was extremely difficult. They locked the wagon wheels so they wouldn't turn; sometimes they dragged trees behind in order to hold the wagons back; often they tied ropes to trees and then untied them one at a time to let a wagon down.

Snow compounded the problem. In Chinook Pass deep snow may persist throughout July, so some of these routes were usable only during brief periods in summer. That must have caused pileups, heavy traffic, and frantic efforts on the part of team drivers.

Perhaps the best-known route to Puget Sound in the early days was the Naches Pass Wagon Road, between Fort Walla Walla to the east and Fort Steilacoom, on Puget Sound. The name Naches was made up of two Indian words, *naugh*, meaning "rough" or "turbulent," and *chez*, meaning "water." The first wagon trains to go through had to lower their wagons over a 30-foot cliff, and the horses were led down a narrow gully. The road came into general use about 1840, but in due course other routes were developed through lower and more convenient passes.

After 1884 the Naches Trail fell into disuse. Though most of it has now returned to nature, State Route 410 follows it some of the way, and there are places where the original route can be seen, as in Federation Forest State Park, about 15 miles west of the Pacific Crest Trail.

We have been seeing Mount Rainier for miles, but now we approach our closest point, 12 miles from the summit, and enter Mount Rainier National Park. Here we begin to get a true feeling of the great massiveness of this volcano, and the awesome number and size of its glaciers and snowfields.

This highest of Cascade Mountains, 14,410 feet, has the longest glacier (5 miles) of any peak in the lower 48 states. Altogether, it has some forty glaciers which cover a total of 35 square miles. Mount

Mount Rainier

Rainier is also the site of record snowfalls. In the winter of 1971–1972 the Paradise Valley weather station recorded over 93 feet, the most ever measured anywhere.

Some spots on the mountain are still warm, and the volcano is believed to be dormant rather than extinct. The last volcanic activity occurred about five hundred years ago. A fact more ominous, perhaps, is that Rainier is susceptible to mud flows; even a small eruption could trigger a devastating river of silt and debris. The Osceola Mudflow, some five thousand years ago, traveled 40 miles down a valley and spread out to blanket 65 square miles under sediments as thick as 70 feet—all where the towns of Enumclaw and Buckley now stand.

Considering all the glacial ice on the mountain, any substantial heating of the rock could cause a melting and production of slurry, the kind associated with the 1965 eruption of Irazú Volcano in Costa Rica. And in the opinion of the U.S. Geological Survey, Mount Rainier could erupt again at any time.

For the present, however, it is peaceful. Thousands of persons climb it each year, up one of the more than forty routes by which the summit has been reached.

Despite the volcanic history, or perhaps because of it, there are groves of trees on the slopes of Rainier that have grown in a serene environment for hundreds of years. The Trail of the Patriarchs is a self-guiding descriptive route through lowland forest where Douglas firs and western redcedars reach as much as 25 feet in circumference, attain a height of almost 300 feet, and are nearly a thousand years old.

The Pacific Crest Trail hiker, accustomed to leaping across the small but vigorous torrents of high mountain streams, finds here that the green-tinted waters have a gentler gradient and flow more silently; but they are tremendously forceful, forming innumerable whirlpools. Vine maple, one of the most abundant plants in these lowland communities, grows along the stream bank, together with western redcedar, the giant with scalelike foliage and reddish-brown fibrous bark.

Unfortunately, most people lack time or patience to roam these woods and appreciate their real character, much less understand the constant play of ecological dramas. White-footed mice eat seeds and are eaten by carnivores, such as martens. Snowshoe hares munch leafy plants and are captured by owls. Ruffed grouse take berries and are taken by bobcats. The aplodontia, a large brown rodent, may be stalked by a coyote even as it consumes vegetation along the streams. There seem to be enough chickarees to plant nuts and reseed the forest. Such endless cycles along much of the Pacific Crest Trail show that life is fairly well balanced.

We enjoy finding and naming parts of these natural communities, but more fundamental satisfaction is to be gained from observing the dynamic day-to-day actions, conflicts, dilemmas. What if the red-shafted flicker fails to find enough insects to eat? Suppose there is a poor berry crop—what do cedar waxwings do? If the population of rodents declines, where does that leave the hawks and owls?

If we could only follow and understand the daily regimen of a single chipmunk, see how it touches the lives of other animals, or find out all that happens if it doesn't dash quickly enough under a shrub to avoid the talons of a swooping hawk, we would have a real key to forest ecology.

But then, as soon as we learn the habits of lowland residents, our trail climbs again in elevation; and with that the environment changes, bit by bit, until it has altered completely in alpine and subalpine regions.

In contrast to dense stands of larch, fir, and pine, the traveler here finds only sparse vegetation, open meadows, and rocky areas. There may be some spruce, a little larch, and familiar whitebark pine, but mostly we see meadows of heather and other bright flowers, and perhaps stunted fir or juniper. Mountain spirea, rock brake and snow lily are characteristic—but only when (or if) the heavy mantle of winter snow is lifted by summer sunshine.

The hiker now descends the other side of the mountains into a drier environment, and not only does the scene change again—to semiarid bunchgrass, ponderosa pine, and sagebrush—but the combinations of animal life change also, and we have to start all over again. The only constants are the natural laws that govern all these habitats.

From Naches Pass the Pacific Crest Trail proceeds for a while in a northeasterly curve and then heads due north from pass to pass—Green, Tacoma, Stampede, Dandy, Yakima, Snoqualmie. From high points the views back south are superlative, especially of Mount Rainier.

Passing clear-cuts, turquoise lakes, and more scenic views, traveling sometimes on knife-edge ridges, sometimes through deep forest, we arrive at Snoqualmie Pass. Where today we hear an all-pervading roar of traffic on Interstate 90, the sounds on a wagon road opened through here in 1868 were the crunch of steel-rimmed wagon wheels on a roadbed of split cedar puncheon. The teamsters who guided and pulled heavy freight wagons over these rudimentary roads, where a misstep could send teams and vehicles into muddy swamps or deep gulches and cause hours of delay, seem scarcely less than Herculean. The freight drivers also had to contend with landslides, fallen trees, washed out roads, and other obstacles.

Today the pass has been much altered. Fire has taken parts of the forest, and human beings have rearranged the contours through highway construction. Whole ridges were sheared off and truncated, streams rechanneled and openings cut out of the woods. Trucks, cars, and buses now cause an almost unceasing roar in the canyons and across the pass day and night, year round. We are at our closest approach to Seattle, which is approximately 50 miles to the west.

The trail passes through a forest of ski lifts. To the west two swaths sweep straight up the peaks to carry wire lines. Not far away are open patches that have been cut bare of trees and installed with a network of logging roads.

Perhaps human beings will some day stop building giant roads and power lines, just as they seem to be stopping the building of giant dams. Perhaps, also, better ways will be found to extract resources of the forest.

Nature tries to cover the scars, largely by forest regrowth, but it is difficult to hide everything. An arrow of industrialization shoots across the trail, and while all this may be essential to human progress, there is growing evidence that trails and wilderness areas are also necessary. Indeed, with the specter of environmental contamination caused by industrialization, we need more wild areas and less commercial encroachment on nature.

Snoqualmie Pass has many chalet homes, condominiums, and "alpine villages," set beneath a backdrop of cliffs that give us the feeling of being in Yosemite Valley or the Swiss Alps. There are also scars of old roads and old developments—cumulative uses unkind to the natural scene.

Sixty-five miles farther on, through the proposed Alpine Lakes Wilderness, we come to Stevens Pass, not as thoroughly altered as Snoqualmie Pass. It has only a power station, service station, restaurant, and ski area on U.S. Route 2.

Stevens Pass was named for the man who scouted out a crossing for a railroad, which was completed through here in 1893. Builders of a railroad in this rough terrain had to overcome two major obstacles: the steep grade and the danger of avalanche. Switchbacks and loop trestles in narrow canyons solved the problem of gaining or losing altitude in a short time, but how could snowslides be controlled?

On March 1, 1910, a passenger train stalled in the snow near here was swept away by a huge avalanche that took 101 lives. After that, a tunnel nearly 8 miles long was drilled through the granite and completed in 1929. Some of the old snow sheds that protected the original tracks can still be seen below the highway.

In Stevens Pass we have granite again, a refreshing sight after so much lava terrain. The region is topographically bold and im-

North Cascades from the air

mense, and even when rain falls and clouds swirl around the mountains, we glimpse cliffs, domes, peaks, patches of snow, and dense forests. These shifting mists let only parts of the view be captured at a time, and we are never sure what will become visible next. Such a drama is one of the benefits of hiking in inclement weather. The clouds may clear away, but even if they do not, certain aspects of travel in the rain—freshness, drops on foliage, cascades everywhere—have their reward.

We have already seen so many falling, tumbling streams that we can appreciate the aptness of the name Cascade Mountains. And now that we come to the North Cascades, where there is greater rainfall and heavy snow, we find more streams and falls than ever.

Some cascades are tremendously violent, though to see these the Pacific Crest Trail hiker may have to descend to points where high country streams take on more water. On the western approach by road to Stevens Pass, for example, is Deception Falls, which plunges through narrow rocky defiles with such turbulence that its roar is deafening and its violence shakes the earth. Great clouds of mist shoot into the air and filter through the trees. In some ways the scene resembles an Oriental silk-screen print, almost unreal because so much water is trying to fall so fast into a small channel and roar on again.

This spectacle, on a smaller scale, is repeated endlessly for the trail hiker at high elevations. However, one should not get the impression that there really is water everywhere in the North Cascades. Sometimes hikers must walk long stretches without water, especially in late summer when some of the side streams cease running. In other cases they follow rivers—but the trail may be hundreds of feet up the wall of the canyon in which the river flows, and hikers can only hear the roar of unseen waters below.

We are now ready to cover the last segment of the Pacific Crest Trail, nearly 200 miles, and there are no stores. One can get supplies by taking side trips off the trail, but the trail no longer touches developed areas except for two road crossings.

This undeveloped domain may seem anomalous in a modern industrial age, but it turns out that this is the way a majority of Washingtonians would like their state to be kept. According to a survey conducted in 1974 by the National Bank of Commerce, most people prefer the state the way it is and do not want any growth during the next ten years. Only 18 percent favored growth. The rest wanted none even though it might mean loss of employment. That, they said, was preferable to urban crowding, deteriorating environment, and related difficulties.

Not long after leaving Stevens Pass, the Pacific Crest Trail enters the Glacier Peak Wilderness, and the hiker now experiences some of the most difficult hiking on the trail. Here the path is most likely to be covered with snow, even in August, and a traveler should expect to slip and slither in places.

The trail curves and zigzags, subjects the hiker to steep climbs, and rises to within a mile of flowing ice systems on the summit of Glacier Peak. There are biting flies, fog drip if mists are flowing, knife-edge ridges, frozen lakes, and fallen trees.

At this latitude of 48 degrees north, the temperatures can be cold in midsummer. The weather may be unpredictable—windy and rainy on the one hand, or stunningly beautiful on the other. If there has been a winter of heavy snow, followed by a spring and summer that have not melted the snowpack rapidly, a traveler may need crampons, ice axes, and sturdy ropes.

But for all the effort, given good weather, the views are eminently worth the price, views not only of Glacier Peak and environs, but of much of the rest of the North Cascades and of Mount Rainier to the south.

We have entered a more complex and confusing mountain system than the ones farther south, where volcanic cones or granite ridges were neatly arranged in nearly straight lines.

From here north, the mountains are split and spread out, a jumbled, seemingly disorganized mass of sedimentary, metamorphic, and granitic rocks with volcanoes. They are also covered with a total of nearly 800 glaciers, owing to the heavy precipitation that comes eastward from the Pacific Ocean. Hence, from here on, we have handsome scenery in all directions, but we must have good maps or know the mountains well to be able to identify them all.

However spectacular the views from open summits, not all hikers can get up that high or win the battle against snow, ice, and wind. For them, the alternatives are to try other trails and plan only to hike toward the Pacific Crest Trail. Even if they never reach it, getting there is half the fun, and they should not be misled by the name Glacier Peak Wilderness. It is not entirely desolate and frozen.

Far from it. If one drives up the Suiattle River, for example, proceeds as far as possible, parks, and then walks another mile, he will cross the river and enter the Glacier Peak Wilderness in as green and luxuriant a forest as any in the North Cascades.

The trees are mostly western redcedar and western hemlock with Douglas fir. On the forest floor grow sphagnum moss, ferns, daisies, yellow buttercups, and pearly everlasting. Rows of young hemlocks grow along downed logs. Limbs of living trees are draped with curtains of moss.

Twinflowers blossom nearly everywhere, sending out long stems by which they propagate themselves. Foliose lichens take over whole slopes, looking like lettuce leaves strewn under the hemlocks. Pip-

Western redcedar forest, Glacier Peak Wilderness

sissewa and pyrola bloom profusely, but the trillium and dwarf dogwood begin to fade in late July.

The glens have a brilliant green hue, the middle layer of vegetation being composed of vine maples. We hop across a stream, only
to hop back and stop to observe the river pebbles: pinkish and
yellow granite, dark schists, specimens shot through with veins of
quartz. It reminds us of the multiple rock types seen in Klamath
Mountain streams of northern California.

A black snake with yellow lines on the sides and top and small
red spots on both sides moves out of our way as we cross the
Suiattle River on a trail bridge.

With that we enter lowlands abundant with salmonberry, blue-
berry, and thimbleberry, all edible. Everything is wet in lower areas
along the river, not only from rain but from the drip of mist. Mosquitoes assail us again. Devil's club is common. We see varied types,
colors, and designs of shelf fungus, laden with water droplets in a
pattern resembling leopard fur.

So heavy is the growth, so steep the ravines and mountain
slopes, that one thinks of Sasquatch, or Bigfoot, the legendary dark-
furred beast supposed to inhabit the Northwest but never captured.
It seems, looking at these forests, that a beast unknown to human
beings could very well be living up here.

As we climb up away from the Suiattle River, the woods become more quiet. The trees are immense. Sunlight breaks through
now and then and illumines the trunks, brightens the lichens, filters
through vine maples, and falls on the forest floor.

Time after time we come to the expanded buttresses of western
redcedar where clefts are filled with spider webs arranged *en echelon*.

We are struck not only with the sheer attractiveness of great
cedar trunks but with the ability of water and nutrients to rise so
high in a tree. We barely have time, as a rule, to recognize a few
of these trailside miracles, and almost no opportunity to give them
the reflection they deserve.

Could we shake off the shackles that bind us to schedules and
itineraries, we might delay, Muir-like, for hours to log into our
minds a few of the complex parts of this forest and what they
might mean. Few scientists or philosophers have explained the central functions of a forest as well as, say, certain cosmic laws have
been explained. We need an Einstein of the woods.

How some of the Douglas firs along the trail can lean so far
without falling is amazing. There are countless holes at the bases of
tree trunks or in fallen trees; and sometimes bits of debris come cascading down from where a chickaree works.

A varied thrush flies through the forest and another sings in the
distance. A pair of woodpeckers sails through the trees. Hummingbirds come down to examine a hiker's red pack.

A side stream plunges down a little ravine, crashing and tumbling, breaking apart and coming together innumerable times, flinging spray, wetting mosses and ferns that line the route, forming pools in which the waters stay only briefly, glistening in the sun, boiling, churning—all icy cold, the best of drinking water.

Later we come to less violent streams whose waters slip musically into pools and fill the dells with bell-like sounds. The waters sift through rotting logs, roots, and branches of hemlocks. Streamside vegetation consists of devil's club and skunk cabbage—the latter with leaves nearly 4 feet long—Sitka valerian, wild lilies of the valley, and Queen's cup.

We get tantalizing glimpses of snow-covered peaks ahead. Although we see few large mammals, we know that deer, at least, are close by because we frequently observe their tracks in muddy patches along the trail.

Suddenly we come out of the trees into a meadow so heavily vegetated that the plants come up to our waist: meadow rue, columbine, tiger lily, and sweetshrub. To the right is a cascading waterfall. Ahead rise the wooded portals of the valley. And above, appearing and disappearing as clouds drift by, are the icy shoulders and rocky promontories of Glacier Peak.

The day has advanced too far to go on, and so we return without reaching the Pacific Crest Trail. But it would have been little use anyway, for we meet three girls who have hiked the trail from the north, their path repeatedly blocked by snow.

Around the western and northern sides of Glacier Peak, the Pacific Crest Trail winds in and out and up and down, crosses the Suiattle River, climbs up forested slopes to Suiattle Pass, and starts the long descent down Agnes Creek to Stehekin River country.

We occasionally dip into shaded, fern-lined ravines and concentrations of giant Alaska cedar, a tree in a completely different genus from that to which the western redcedar belongs. They are easy to distinguish because the drooping foliage gives them a wilted appearance. Alaska cedars seem to prefer a somewhat drier environment, though they are found in moist glades.

The cedar dells along the shady north-facing slope of Agnes Creek are so filled with them that this part of the Pacific Crest Trail could well be called the Avenue of Giants.

Crossing a bridge above the white water of Agnes Creek, we shortly arrive in Stehekin River country. But anyone thinking that so peaceful a valley must have a peaceful river is thoroughly mistaken. The Stehekin River is violent, churning, and awesomely powerful: leaping over rocks, swirling with enormous crashing force against walls, carrying trunks and logs downstream, tearing away

Wood fern, Glacier Peak Wilderness

whole sections of land. But where it is not foamy white from all the turbulence, it is a rich turquoise or emerald green, one of the most beautiful of Cascade streams.

The trail passes through part of Lake Chelan National Recreation Area and North Cascades National Park. This section is reached by primitive road, and a local bus service takes passengers from a boat landing on Lake Chelan up the Stehekin Valley toward Cascade Pass.

The temporary routing of the Pacific Crest Trail follows the road for a time, then plunges into the woods again for a rise along Bridge Creek. On this eastern side of the Cascade Range one finds a drier environment, the moisture having fallen mostly on the Cascades to the west. The Pacific slopes may get more than 500 inches of snow a year, but the drying winds that sweep down into the Stehekin Valley country bring less than a fifth as much snow.

We still have cool and shady glens with ferns almost shoulder high, perhaps air-conditioned by a roaring icy stream. But then we can round a corner and in open sunlight find temperatures close to 100 degrees. Though the land is dry, we have at last apparently left the region of poison oak.

What strikes us is the greater number of wild animals seen in this area. Mammals include deer, chipmunks, golden-mantled ground squirrels, and bears. Conies live in rock piles.

Contrary to what we saw on the Suiattle side of the Glacier Peak Wilderness, these woods are full of birds. Most obvious are woodpeckers traveling from tree to tree. Wrens and thrushes sing complicated songs, while vireos sound their simple notes persistently. Flycatchers also chirp in monotones.

On a day's hike we see at least half a dozen warblers, but they are much more silent. Finches, juncos, and chipping sparrows hop in the shrubbery near the trail.

Out of the shadows a slow-moving form emerges onto the trail: a female blue grouse. At this time of year she is bound to have chicks back in the thicket, and sure enough, one by one, they cross the trail to join her.

Just as we come to an open place and observe the brilliant reddish bark of a tall lone ponderosa pine, a black-red-yellow western tanager flies out of the tree and across a glade. Few natural color combinations are as sharply visible as those of that bird in that tree.

Along the stream we find other forms of life: for example, a water snake probes among the boulders just above the splash line.

We might have missed this had we been distance-eaters scrambling for miles; on this trail it pays to go slowly.

Coming up to Rainy Pass, we are reminded by the name that

Foliose lichen, Glacier Peak Wilderness

the Cascades are not as dry in summer as the Sierra Nevada, and
that storms can be expected at any time. When the clouds are gone,
though, these mountains appear in all their immensity and beauty.

To the west now rise the most rugged parts of North Cascades
National Park, especially the Pickett Range, 25 miles away. These
mountains mainly consist of highly resistant granitic gneiss, which
erodes into hardrock spires, sharp peaks, and knife ridges. The range
is heavily glaciated, with scores of alpine lakes.

Though hundreds of miles of side trails reach into remote
parts of this park and adjacent mountain recreation areas, the land
is so rugged that travelers should pay special attention to safety. For
instance, they should read twice this sign along the trail:

> Caution. Trail hazards. Back country snow and stream
> crossings may be hazardous during spring and early summer.
> Bridges or footlogs are not always available. Water levels begin
> to rise in mornings and during rainy seasons so use caution when
> fording streams. When fording, release waist strap on pack
> and rope yourself to a companion on the stream bank. Be alert
> for unstable snow conditions. Avalanche snow over water
> courses is often undercut, and questionable snow bridges or
> fields should be probed with a walking stick or ice axe.

This region offers good opportunities for one- and two-day
hikes, such as going from Rainy Pass down to Lake Chelan, then on
to the town of Chelan by boat.

And a great deal can be said for loop trips: hiking in and out
the same way on the same day. You go in with the sun in the morning, and on returning have an afternoon sun which changes the
shadows, forms, and views. A waterfall subdued by shade in the
morning tumbles in full light during the afternoon. Different life
forms may be seen, some perhaps engaged in different activities.

After such a day we are inclined to believe John Burroughs:
"To find new things, take the path you took yesterday."

Approaching the end of the Pacific Crest Trail, and perhaps the
end of a summer's hiking, we begin to look a little nostalgically
on the simple things that came to mean so much. Like the coming
of dawn.

Light begins to be perceived about four in the morning, sil-
houetting the eastern peaks. Of course, if we are in a secluded camping spot in some sheltered ravine, it may be six hours before sunlight reaches that point. Vague, unidentifiable wildlife sounds are
heard in the distance, or perhaps the call of a thrush coming up from
the canyon below. Snowclad summits receive the initial glimmers
of purple, then red, then orange, the whole eventually becoming a
mass of blue and gold. Tufts or streamers of cloud curl over the

Pasayten Wilderness

shoulders of ridges, but these may disappear in an hour or two. If they don't, keep your rain jacket handy.

After a while the wind rises, and the tranquillity of the woods gives way to thrashing limbs that sound like an orchestral concert of stringed instruments.

North of Rainy Pass and the newly completed North Cascades Highway, the Pacific Crest Trail enters the Pasayten Wilderness, through which it passes for the rest of the distance to the Canadian boundary.

Views continue to be spectacular as the trail rises and falls between 4,000 and 7,200 feet. The character of the land changes from granitic rock to sedimentary, and we have shale, sandstone, and conglomerate—rock types rather rare along the trail.

The terrain on this final stretch is rough glaciated country with alpine valleys and lakes. Vegetation in high places is composed of spruce, fir, and larch, sometimes in scrubby form because of the battle against the elements, hence the names Rainy Pass, Windy Pass, and Foggy Pass. At lower elevations, Douglas fir, hemlock, and white pine grow in places subject to the destructive violence of avalanches.

The Pasayten Wilderness, a mountainous preserve of 505,524 acres, summarizes the environments of the Cascades. It has nearly all major rock types, has been glaciated, and is endowed with sheer walls, high peaks, waterfalls, and deep, dense forests.

One hikes beside willow and alder along the streams. In high country, naked except for carpeting wildflowers, grow lupine and paintbrush by the acre, with a background skyline of sharply pointed peaks.

Most trails follow stream courses and pass some of the nearly one hundred lakes in the wilderness. In other localities grow open forests of ponderosa pine. Mammals that one may encounter include deer, bear, coyotes, bobcats, porcupines, and mountain goats.

And then, at last, the Pacific Crest Trail reaches Monument 78, on the border between Canada and the United States. And here it ends; or does it? The route continues north into Manning Provincial Park, itself a sizable reserve of 176,000 acres administered by the British Columbia Department of Recreation and Conservation.

This brings us to country of beaver, muskrat, and moose, and an introduction to the millions of acres of wild country in British Columbia and the Canadian Rockies.

Coming down Castle Creek to Manning Park Lodge, ranger station, campground, and other "conveniences of civilization," we find ourselves on Canadian Route 3, ready for a return to the other world.

The trip is over—but we shall be years sorting and resorting the memories of it. We resolve to return whenever possible—to get "recharged" again, to visit favorite haunts, to try out segments missed or never seen. We have really only begun.

Hikers having sampled the Pacific Crest Trail and being in first-class physical condition are in an excellent position to try out other trails—if there are any near home. If not, the mandate is clear: trails are very often fought for and brought into being by dedicated hikers who know what hiking is all about and the kinds of country trails ought to go through. Exposure to the outdoors should build up wider human resolve to rectify errors of the past and make the earth a more pleasant place on which to live.

Having gone through miles of wind and wood, the hiker knows what perfection can be, and would well understand the words of Chief Seattle, leader of the Suquamish Tribe in Washington Territory in 1854:

"This we know. The earth does not belong to man; man belongs to the earth. . . . So if we sell you our land, love it as we've loved it. Care for it as we've cared for it. Hold in your mind the memory of the land as it is when you take it. And with all your strength, with all your mind, with all your heart, preserve it for your children, and love it . . . as God loves us all."

Pacific Crest Trail in Desolation Wilderness, California

10

Where Next?

GIVEN THE EXPLOSIVE increase in numbers of backpackers, bicyclers, horseback riders, and other trail users, the need for a wider variety and larger number of trails is evident. Hence the future of long-distance trails seems to be one of expansion, but not without problems. As we have seen, Americans have threatened to love some of their trails and wilderness areas to death, at least where public use is uncontrolled, and there are abundant conflicts over which trails should be used by whom.

The Bureau of Outdoor Recreation, U.S. Department of the Interior, after discovering that walking for pleasure was increasing in popularity faster than any other major outdoor activity, helped in 1968 to draft Public Law 10-543, the National Trails System Act.

This act focused on three main categories of trails: national scenic trails, national recreation trails, and connecting or side trails. Criteria were set up for each category so that the establishment of new trails could be better coordinated.

As we have seen, two trails were initially designated as National Scenic Trails: the Appalachian Trail and the Pacific Crest Trail. Several other proposed long trails are under study for inclusion in the national system.

One is the Potomac Heritage Trail, an 825-mile route from the mouth of the Potomac River between Maryland and Virginia to its sources in Pennsylvania and West Virginia, including the 170-mile Chesapeake and Ohio Canal towpath, already heavily used by hikers and bicyclers.

A fourth trail for which preliminary studies are complete and recommendations made to Congress is the North Country Trail, which would extend about 3,400 miles from a junction with the Appalachian Trail in Vermont through the states of New York, Pennsylvania, Ohio, Michigan, Wisconsin, and Minnesota to a junction with the Lewis and Clark Trail in North Dakota. An advantage of this long trail would be that it is located within a half day's drive of about one half of the nation's people. The dominant factor in routing the North Country Trail was the inclusion of the most scenic portions of each state. Task-force members who studied the route recognized that it would bisect a panorama of American history from the period of exploration and colonial settlement to the eras of lumbering, canal construction, railroads, and land settlement by pioneers on their westward trek.

At this writing, the planning of a Continental Divide Trail is also nearing completion. This 3,100-mile path would extend from near the Mexican boundary in southwestern New Mexico along the Continental Divide to the Canadian border in Glacier National Park. Because of its location along the crests of many spectacular mountains, it would in all likelihood become popular much as the Pacific Crest Trail has.

Citizens are at work identifying and promoting other trails. They do this by hiking certain routes and then encouraging lawmakers to carry their proposals through the legislative process. For example, bills have been introduced in Congress to establish an east-west Pacific Northwest National Scenic Trail, approximately 1,000 miles long, between the continental divide in Glacier National Park, Montana, and Pacific Ocean beaches in Olympic National Park, Washington.

Other scenic trail systems under study include the Oregon Trail, the Lewis and Clark Trail, the Santa Fe Trail, and the Mormon Trail.

But according to Bureau of Outdoor Recreation officials, the greatest priority for the future will be the establishment of national recreational trails near large urban centers. Whereas longer scenic trails are generally closed to motor vehicles, shorter recreation trails are intended to accommodate a wide variety of users. As of 1975, 46 trails have been designated as National Recreation Trails in 22 states and the District of Columbia. The longest is 28 miles and the shortest 1,200 feet. Some are only for persons on bicycles or foot; others are for snowmobiles in winter and bicycles in summer; one is for blind persons, several for wheelchair travelers, and a large number for horseback riders. These are likely to become very popular, and will generate demands for more.

Criteria set by the National Trails System Act must be met before any route receives recognition as a national recreation trail. Such criteria include readiness for public use before designation, proximity to an urban area, and an administering agency to assure that the trail will be available for public use at least ten consecutive years after designation.

According to federal recreation officials, some people do not want their favorite hiking trails to become nationally recognized for fear that this will mean greater use. Other people, however, are eager for the publicity and increased use stimulated by such national recognition. Still others believe that the best way to success is to make hiking, wilderness areas, and trails so widely known and admired that it would be unthinkable to reduce them.

Several regional periodicals specializing in the outdoors keep hikers informed about trail matters and environmental affairs. One such is the *Signpost, Newsletter for the Northwest Outdoors*, available from Signpost Publications, 16812 36th Avenue West, Lynnwood, Washington, 98036. Camp Research Foundation also issues a newsletter, the *Pacific Crest Trail Quarterly*, which gives an abundance of details not only on trail conditions but on hiking, riding, club meetings, conservation, historical data, supplies, and equipment.

William Kemsley, publisher of *Backpacker Magazine*, observes that the number of hikers has multiplied while the miles of trails available to them have diminished, owing to suburban sprawl. He calls for stepped-up publicity and additional trails, appealing for solutions more sensible than trying to keep backpacking secret. "The solution that seemed most obvious to me," he concluded, "was to build more trails to relieve the congestion."

Furthermore, he urges backpackers themselves to get out and do the building, much as their predecessors did. If that happened, he feels, "we would quickly alleviate overcrowding." If this is not done, some of the prime terrain will be taken over by snowmobilers, motorcyclers, and others who are getting more and more powerful through organization and through their favorable impact on sales of equipment. This could lead to an unbalanced situation, since there are more walkers, hikers, and backpackers than there are snowmobilers, motorboaters, trailer campers, and hunters combined.

The crux of the matter is that hiking is one of the least expensive forms of recreation. Since hikers therefore do not buy machines to propel themselves along, they do not have the intense Congressional lobbying of large motor companies behind them when the time comes to build more trails or reserve new wilderness areas.

In any case, many people are hard at work, not only in the

United States but abroad. Some national recreation trails are administered by city, county, or state park agencies; others by federal agencies such as the Bureau of Land Management; and still others by private organizations, such as the several trails set aside by the Bowaters Southern Paper Company in Tennessee.

In foreign countries steps are also being taken to increase opportunities for trail users. After standing on the Appalachian Trail in May, 1968, Michio Oi, then chief of the planning section of the Japanese National Parks Bureau, returned to Japan to help establish the 840-mile-long Tokai Nature Trail, between Mount Takao, on the outskirts of Tokyo, and Mount Mino-o, in the western suburbs of Osaka. The trail incorporates areas of historic interest and scenic beauty, including lakes, temples, a battlefield, and an ancient castle. Spontaneous support by the Japanese people has led to suggestions for similar trails in Hokkaido, Kyushu, and Shikoku.

The famed Milford Track, on New Zealand's South Island, winds through huge chasms and among sheer mountain walls to terminate in the spectacular Fiordland National Park.

In England, besides the 250-mile long Pennine Way, which was the first long-distance footpath to be completed there, 11 other routes for hikers, cyclists, and/or horseback riders have been approved by the Minister of Housing and Local Government and are in various stages of completion. Second to be established was the Cleveland Way, a continuous footpath nearly 100 miles long, which runs in a roughly horseshoe shape along the borders of the North York Moors National Park. The Cleveland Way combines in about equal proportions sections of exceptional moorland scenery with some of the highest cliffs on the eastern coast of England.

Also completed is England's first long-distance bridle path, the South Downs Way, extending for 80 miles between Eastbourne and the Hampshire border, mostly along the ridge of the South Downs in an area of outstanding natural beauty. This bridleway may also be used by hikers and bicyclers.

An interesting feature of the English system is that the government makes no attempt to acquire lands traversed by these trails. It simply oversees the hiker's or rider's access to lands where trails have existed for centuries, asking only that the user treat private property with respect and refrain from crossing farmers' fields or leaving open any gate that was found closed.

Canada's trail system is also progressing. Plans have been drawn up for the Acadian Trail, which will continue northward from the Appalachian Trail through Nova Scotia and New Brunswick. Proposed in 1970 by the Maritime Region of the Canadian Youth Hostel Association, the Acadian Trail already encompasses 60 miles of coastline. Eventually this will become part of a trans-Canada hiking trail system.

Columbian ground squirrel

Another segment of such a system already exists for 430 miles along the Niagaran escarpment: The Bruce Trail, from Queenston to Tobermory, in southern Ontario. That path may eventually be linked with the Finger Lakes Trail System of New York State and then with the Appalachian Trail to create a 2,000-mile-long route from Georgia to the tip of the Bruce Peninsula.

This is just a sampling of new trails being established worldwide. It shows that on an international scale the number of paths available for hiking, bicycling, horseback riding, and other uses seems to be on the increase. But many supporters and administrators are concerned that money appropriated at different levels of government seems a mere pittance compared to the need for more trails. In this connection the recent experience of snowmobile trails should be instructive. First, local clubs of snowmobilers were formed. These merged into federations of increasing size that influenced legislation at various levels of state governments. Written into law were provisions that required parts of snowmobile registration fees to be applied toward building new snowmobile trails and constructing facilities, thus assuring more trails for snowmobile users in the future.

One snowmobile company has also developed a rig that "grooms" the snow to keep it in proper condition for use, thus encouraging snowmobilers to stay on designated trails. Despite construction of tens of thousands of miles of snowmobile trails in the past few years, industry manufacturers feel that this is only a small percentage of what is needed. In some places considerable summertime use of snowmobile trails as foot trails has developed.

Meanwhile, at public and private levels, proposals have been considered for the establishment of a nationwide network of trails so that Americans afoot can hike from one part of the United States to any other. One proposal envisions major trails passing through each state, Canada, and Mexico, combining bits of North American history with samplings of wild scenery.

At a recent National Trails Conference participants from all sections of the United States and Canada met to discuss the trail "crunch" and to make proposals for the future. Besides recommending that trail budgets of federal agencies be increased, the council urged that full funding from the Land and Water Conservation Fund be made available to federal and state agencies for trail building.

Other suggestions for the future included the establishment of local trail councils and, probably most important, meetings of trail groups on a local level to solve differences and conflicts over use and development of trails. As the National Trails Council points out, given the overcrowding of existing trails and the urgent need for additional ones, "Can we really afford the luxury of user-group conflicts?"

Mountain stream in Glacier Peak Wilderness, Washington

Meanwhile, what's ahead for the Pacific Crest Trail? Are there plans to extend it north into British Columbia, or south into Baja California?

Well, there has been a plan circulating since 1943 to build a trail from the highest mountain in North America, Mount McKinley, to the highest in South America, Mount Aconcagua, a distance of about 10,000 miles. And a logical extension of that idea is to build a trail all the way from Bering Strait to the Straits of Magellan, an estimated 20,000 miles. Some day it may be done. Each government would have responsibility for its own section of such a trail, and those projects are likely to have low priority for a while. Even in the United States there is a great deal of work yet to be done in completing the Pacific Crest Trail.

Nevertheless, such dreams are necessary, especially for visionaries who have traditionally become the heroes of hiking movements around the world.

Even though the Pacific Crest Trail is not yet completed, hikers by the thousands are using it, together with associated side trails, parks, forests, and wilderness areas. If the trail is sometimes crowded, let us take at least some comfort. People clamoring to get out among the snow-capped peaks, rich rain forests, and flowering deserts should help to assure that there will always be a Pacific Crest Trail.

Appendix 1

Your Wilderness Trip

*The richest values of wilderness lie not
in the days of Daniel Boone nor even in the
present, but rather in the future.*

Aldo Leopold

THE PACIFIC NORTHWEST REGION of the United States Forest Service
has issued a folder which summarizes current advice of value to
wilderness users. Because of its value to hikers on the Pacific Crest
Trail as well, it is reprinted here almost in its entirety.

The Wilderness and You

The U.S. Forest Service provides a special type of outdoor experience when you visit a National Forest Wilderness. These special
areas, established by the Wilderness Act of September 3, 1964, are
managed so as to offer solitude in a pristine and natural setting for
present and future generations.

The perpetuation of the Wilderness environment is largely dependent upon the behavior of the user. Most of the public is highly
sensitive to environmental quality, ecological factors, and opportunities for spiritual benefit in pristine Wilderness. They recognize
that a Wilderness is sensitive to the presence of man who is a visitor,
and does not remain.

In some locations, however, increasing numbers of visitors, and
improper behavior by some, threaten the environmental value and
quality of the Wilderness resource. There is a need to control use.
Therefore, the Forest Service has adopted a permit system which can
be used in the future to limit use as the need arises. The permit
system will help the Forest Service obtain important use data which

can be used to improve Wilderness management, and will afford an opportunity for the Forest Officer to give advice on your Wilderness trip. The informed user is always more responsive to the environmental quality of National Forest Wilderness.

A wilderness permit is required for each trip involving overnight use to the Mt. Jefferson and Three Sisters Wildernesses in Oregon and the Glacier Peak, Goat Rocks, Mt. Adams and Pasayten Wildernesses in Washington.

Permits may be obtained free from various Forest Service offices if your trip originates in a National Forest Wilderness. If you begin your trip in the North Cascades National Park Service complex, obtain a permit from the local offices of the National Park Service. The permit must be in the possession of the group leader during your visit.

The true Wilderness enthusiast expects to find a basic quality in all areas he may visit: solitude. This means different things to different people, but mainly it means freedom from the intrusion of unnatural sights, sounds, and odors.

The response of each individual varies widely, but for the most part, a wilderness experience is psychologically and spiritually fulfilling.

Respect the solitude by avoiding boisterous conduct and loud noises that are disruptive to others. Discharging firearms is discouraged except in hunting season. (The possession or use of firearms is prohibited in National Parks.) The use of motors or motorized vehicles of any sort is expressly forbidden in all areas of the National Wilderness Preservation System.

Wilderness know-how—twelve keys to survival

1. Do not travel alone. Recommended minimum party size is four.
2. Have proper equipment.
3. Plan your trip. Tell family or friends of plan, and follow it.
4. Familiarize yourself with the area from a map. Carry map and a compass.
5. Be in good physical condition. Do not overextend yourself.
6. Be weatherwise. Wetness and wind increase body heat loss (hypothermia) and reduce your chances of survival.
7. Make camp, emergency or otherwise, in a sheltered place, before dark. . . .
8. Travel only in daylight hours.
9. Camp near water, if possible. Some sources of drinking water may be impure. When in doubt, use water purification tablets or boil water for 10 minutes.
10. If you think you are lost keep calm. Take it easy, and do not

panic. Sit down and figure out where you are. Use your head, not your legs.

11. Sudden mountain storms are common, especially in the after-noon and evening. During lightning storms, stay off ridges, away from open meadows, and away from isolated trees. If possible, find shelter among dense, small trees in low areas. If this is not possible, lie down on the ground.
12. Three of anything (shots, whistles, smokes, fires) are a sign of distress. If seen or heard, help will soon be on the way. (Use these three signals only in emergencies.)

Ten essentials

These should be carried on all trips into the Wilderness, winter or summer.

1. Whistle.
2. Map.
3. Compass.
4. Flashlight.
5. Extra food, clothing, and light plastic tarp.
6. Fire starter (candle).
7. First-aid kit.
8. Pocket knife.
9. Sunburn protection and dark glasses.
10. Waterproof matches.

The environment

Your presence, and that of others, has an impact on many en-vironmental factors. The adverse effects can be minimized if all Wilderness visitors understand the biological community of which they are a part.

Man is a temporary visitor who should leave no permanent im-print. The forces of nature must be allowed to continue to dominate the landscape.

The visitor must behave in a responsible manner much as he would if visiting the home of a respected friend. "Tread lightly" on the scene. Avoid leaving your mark as much as possible. Nature will perpetuate itself and replenish itself if given the chance.

Constant use of the same campsites tends to damage the scene. Soils become compacted, campfire ashes accumulate, and firewood is depleted. The site becomes worn which detracts from the ap-pearance.

The vegetation

The trees, shrubs, forbs and grasses are important parts of the mountain biological community. In addition to providing shelter and food for wildlife, the vegetation clothes the slopes, prevents erosion and contributes to esthetic values. Help protect this resource.

Firewood is often scarce, particularly in some of the more popular high mountain areas. Conserve it by keeping your warming and cooking fires small. Burn only dead wood. Many visitors select campsites in lesser-used locations not only for the seclusion, but also because of the greater availability of firewood. The dispersion of overnight campers is encouraged. Portable stoves, canned heat, heat tabs and similar products are efficient and should be used when possible.

Avoid destroying, defacing or carving on growing trees and shrubs, and other natural features! Do not use boughs for beds or shelter. Collecting live plant material is forbidden except by special written permit from the Forest Service.

Party size

Plan your party size to limit groups to no more than 20 people and/or 20 pack and saddle stock. Large groups are destructive to Wilderness. Limits may be in effect for the area you will be visiting. Check with the officer who issues your permit if your party is large.

Horses and pack stock

Many Wilderness visitors travel with horses or other livestock or use the services of commercial packers. Because livestock grazing can seriously damage areas with limited amounts of forage, special requirements on picketing, hobbling, and providing stock feed may be in effect in certain National Forest Wilderness and National Park areas. Check with the local offices of the Forest Service or Park Service on any special rules or closures which may apply to livestock use.

Back packing

This is the most popular and economical way to get into the Wilderness. It is strenuous, but has certain advantages including a wider choice of routes and campsites. Proper equipment (of maximum utility and minimum weight), good physical condition, and careful planning are necessary for enjoyable backpacking. The most important items of equipment include good, comfortable footwear, your pack, and sleeping bag. A down sleeping bag, comfortable to a temperature of 25° F., is ideal.

Menus for back-country packing trips require careful planning. They must be simple but nutritious and substantial, and light in weight. Some hikers prefer to test their menus at home. Meals should be easily prepared with minimum equipment. Many basic dehydrated foods are available at any grocery store, and specialized items are found in sporting goods stores. Backpackers should be able to get by with 1½ pounds (dry weight) of food per day.

Leave canned and bottled foods at home. They are heavy, and you are required to carry out empty cans, bottles, and foil. Repackage items such as sugar, cereal, and dry milk in plastic bags. This saves weight and they fit easily into your pack. Burn the plastic or take it home when you leave. Don't count on catching and eating fish. If the fish are not biting, neither will you.

Don't load yourself down with heavy, unnecessary items and gadgets. Leave your axe and heavy frying pan at home. With carefully selected equipment and food, you should not have to carry more than 30 pounds for a week's trip.

Small, lightweight gas stoves are convenient to cook meals on where firewood is scarce. These stoves and their fuel supply are compact and can be easily carried in your pack.

Get in shape by taking weekend hikes and exercising with full pack. Even then, take it easy the first day or two. Remember that high elevations may cause "altitude sickness" because there is less oxygen in the air. Walk slowly and steadily, and, from time to time, eat some candy or other quick energy food.

Fires in the wilderness

Forest fires are a severe threat to all Wilderness values. Every visitor must be extremely cautious when using fire. Smoking while traveling is forbidden, so be sure to stop in a safe place if you must smoke. Select a safe place to build your campfire. Your fire should be built only in a prepared "bed" where all wood, leaves and other burnable material have been cleared away. Find a spot that is sheltered from the winds, and keep your fire small. Never leave your fire until you are certain it is completely out. When extinguishing your campfire, mix the hot coals with soil and water, stir it completely. Feel the ashes with your hands to be sure the coals are cold throughout.

Each party traveling with pack or saddle stock is required to have an axe, shovel and water bucket.

If special fire restrictions are in effect, the issuing office will advise you.

Waste disposal

There are a number of simple rules for waste disposal that will assure a quality Wilderness now and in the future.

Cans, bottles, metal foil and other refuse must be packed out. Do not bury your trash. Paper and other burnable material should be burned. Don't litter the trail. Put gum and candy wrappers and other similar material in your pocket while traveling. Everyone could help maintain a litter-free Wilderness if each person would pick up trash which may have been thoughtlessly discarded by others.

There are no toilet facilities provided in the Wilderness. Select a spot well away from streams, lakes, camp areas and trails. Cover wastes with soil or rocks.

Most foodstuffs and kitchen wastes of an organic nature will decompose rapidly or be consumed by various organisms including insects and small animals. However, burn as much of this material as possible, and dispose of the rest away from lakes, streams, camp-sites and routes of travel. Better yet, pack it out. Trenchings and diggings are unsightly and may contribute to soil erosion. Limit your digging activities to that needed to prepare your campfire "bed" or to cover or dispose of body wastes.

Do not use soap or detergent in streams or lakes. Keep wash water, fish entrails, garbage and other trash well away from all bodies of water.

You should find a pollution-free environment wherever you may travel in a Wilderness. Do your part to keep it that way by properly disposing of waste materials.

Special regulations for national parks only

Guns, loaded or unloaded, are prohibited.

Dogs or cats are not permitted in any of the back-country of the parks—not even on a leash.

Fishing is allowed under State law, but shooting or molesting any bird or other animal is prohibited.

Appendix 2

**Addresses of Public Agencies Administering Lands
Along or Near the Pacific Crest Trail ***

Supervisor, Cleveland National Forest, 3211 Fifth Avenue, San Diego, California 92103.

Area Manager, Cuyamaca Rancho State Park, Cuyamaca Star Route, Julian, California 92036.

Superintendent, Mt. San Jacinto Wilderness State Park, Box 308, Idyllwild, California 92349.

Supervisor, San Bernardino National Forest, 144 North Mountain View Avenue, San Bernardino, California 92408.

Supervisor, Angeles National Forest, 150 South Los Robles, Pasadena, California 91101.

Supervisor, Sequoia National Forest, 900 West Grand Avenue, Porterville, California 93257.

Superintendent, Sequoia–Kings Canyon National Parks, Three Rivers, California 93271.

Supervisor, Inyo National Forest, 2957 Birch Street, Bishop, California 93514.

Supervisor, Sierra National Forest, 1130 O Street, Fresno, California 93721.

Superintendent, Yosemite National Park, California 95389.

Supervisor, Stanislaus National Forest, 175 South Fairview Lane, Sonora, California 95370.

Supervisor, Toiyabe National Forest, Box 1331, Reno, Nevada 89504.

Supervisor, Eldorado National Forest, 100 Forni Road, Placerville, California 95667.

Supervisor, Tahoe National Forest, Highway 49 and Coyote, Nevada City, California 95959.

* Listed in south-to-north order.

Supervisor, Plumas National Forest, 159 Lawrence Street, Quincy, California 95971.

Supervisor, Lassen National Forest, 707 Nevada Street, Susanville, California 96130.

Superintendent, Lassen Volcanic National Park, Mineral, California 96063.

Area Manager, McArthur–Burney Falls State Park, Route 1, Box 1260, Burney, California 96013.

Supervisor, Shasta-Trinity National Forests, 1615 Continental Street, Redding, California 96001.

Superintendent, Castle Crags State Park, Castella, California 96017.

Supervisor, Klamath National Forest, 1215 South Main Street, Yreka, California 96097.

Supervisor, Winema National Forest, Post Office Building, Klamath Falls, Oregon 97601.

Supervisor, Rogue River National Forest, Box 520, Medford, Oregon 97501.

Superintendent, Crater Lake National Park, Crater Lake, Oregon 97604.

Supervisor, Umpqua National Forest, P.O. Box 1008, Roseburg, Oregon 97470.

Supervisor, Deschutes National Forest, 211 East Revere Street, Bend, Oregon 97701.

Supervisor, Willamette National Forest, Box 10607, 210 East Eleventh Avenue, Eugene, Oregon 97401.

Supervisor, Mount Hood National Forest, 2440 S.E. 195th Avenue, Portland, Oregon 97233.

Supervisor, Gifford Pinchot National Forest, Box 449, Vancouver, Washington 98660.

Supervisor, Snoqualmie–Mt. Baker National Forests, Seattle, Washington 98104.

Superintendent, Mount Rainier National Park, Longmire, Washington 98397.

Supervisor, Wenatchee National Forest, P.O. Box 811, Wenatchee, Washington 98801.

Superintendent, North Cascades National Park, Sedro Wooley, Washington 98284.

Supervisor, Okanogan National Forest, Okanogan, Washington 98840.

Regional Supervisor, Manning Provincial Park, Manning Park, British Columbia.

Appendix 3

Maps and Where to Get Them

THE 22 TOPOGRAPHIC maps listed below, at a scale of 1:250,000, give an overview of the topography of the Pacific Crest Trail route, as well as the surroundings for many miles on each side. More detailed U.S. Geological Survey maps, such as quadrangles, may be selected by consulting state topographic index maps. All topographic maps west of the Mississippi River may be obtained from the U.S. Geological Survey, Central Region—Map Distribution, Denver Federal Center, Building 41, Denver, Colorado 80225. One should remember that these topographic maps do not show the Pacific Crest Trail.

More localized maps issued by the U.S. Forest Service and the National Park Service may be obtained by writing to the addresses given in Appendix 2.

1. San Diego, California
2. Santa Ana, California
3. San Bernardino, California
4. Los Angeles, California
5. Bakersfield, California
6. Trona, California
7. Fresno, California
8. Mariposa, California–Nevada
9. Walker Lake, Nevada–California
10. Sacramento, California
11. Chico, California–Nevada
12. Susanville, California
13. Alturas, California–Oregon
14. Weed, California–Oregon
15. Medford, Oregon–California

16. Roseburg, Oregon
17. Crescent, Oregon
18. Bend, Oregon
19. The Dalles, Oregon–Washington
20. Yakima, Washington
21. Wenatchee, Washington
22. Concrete, Washington

Bibliography

Atkeson, Ray. *The Cascade Range, Northwest Heritage*. Portland, Ore.: Charles H. Belding, 1969.

Baldwin, Ewart M. *Geology of Oregon*. Ann Arbor, Mich.: Edwards Brothers, Inc., 1964.

Brower, David, Ed. *Gentle Wilderness, The Sierra Nevada*. San Francisco: Sierra Club, 1964.

Bullard, Oral, and Lowe, Don. *Short Trips and Trails: The Columbia Gorge*. Beaverton, Ore.: The Touchstone Press, 1974.

Clappe, Louise. *The Shirley Letters from the California Mines, 1851–1852*. New York: Alfred A. Knopf, 1961.

Clarke, Clinton C. *The Pacific Crest Trailway*. Pasadena, Calif.: Pacific Crest Trail System Conference, 1945.

Downs, Theodore. *Fossil Vertebrates of Southern California*. Berkeley and Los Angeles, Calif: University of California Press, 1968.

Farquhar, Francis P. *History of the Sierra Nevada*. Berkeley, Calif.: University of California Press, 1969.

Ferris, Charles M. *Hiking the Oregon Skyline*. Beaverton, Ore.: The Touchstone Press, 1973.

Fisher, Vardis, and Holmes, Opal L. *Gold Rushes and Mining Camps of the Early American West*. Caldwell, Ida.: The Caxton Printers, 1968.

Fried, John J. *Life Along the San Andreas Fault*. New York: Saturday Review Press, 1973.

Gray, William R., *The Pacific Crest Trail*. Washington: The National Geographic Society, 1975.

Harbaugh, John W. *Geology Field Guide to Northern California*. Dubuque, Ia.: William C. Brown Co., 1974.

Hayden, Mike. *Guidebook to the Lake Tahoe Country, Volumes I and II*. Los Angeles: Ward Ritchie Press, 1971.

Horn, Elizabeth L. *Wildflowers 1, The Cascades.* Beaverton, Ore.: The Touchstone Press, 1972.

King, Clarence. *Mountaineering in the Sierra Nevada.* Philadelphia: J. B. Lippincott Company, 1963.

Kirk, Ruth. *Exploring Mount Rainier.* Seattle: University of Washington Press, 1968.

Kroeber, Theodora, and Heizer, Robert F. *Almost Ancestors: The First Californians.* San Francisco: Sierra Club, 1968.

Lavender, David S. *California: Land of New Beginnings.* New York: Harper and Row, 1973.

————. *Land of Giants: The Drive to the Pacific Northwest, 1750– 1950.* Garden City, N.Y.: Doubleday and Company, 1958.

Leadabrand, Russ. *A Guidebook to the Mojave Desert of California.* Los Angeles: Ward Ritchie Press, 1970.

————. *Guidebook to the Mountains of San Diego and Orange Counties.* Los Angeles: Ward Ritchie Press, 1971.

————. *A Guidebook to the San Bernardino Mountains of California.* Los Angeles: Ward Ritchie Press, 1969.

————. *A Guidebook to the San Gabriel Mountains of California.* Los Angeles: Ward Ritchie Press, 1970.

————. *Guidebook to the San Jacinto Mountains of Southern California.* Los Angeles: Ward Ritchie Press, 1971.

————. *A Guidebook to the Southern Sierra Nevada.* Los Angeles: Ward Ritchie Press, 1968.

Le Conte, Joseph. *A Journal of Ramblings Through the High Sierra of California.* New York: Ballantine Books, 1971.

Lowe, Don and Roberta. *100 Northern California Hiking Trails.* Beaverton, Ore.: The Touchstone Press, 1970.

————. *100 Oregon Hiking Trails.* Portland, Ore.: The Touchstone Press, 1969.

McKee, Bates. *Cascadia: The Geologic Evolution of the Pacific Northwest.* New York: McGraw-Hill Book Company, 1972.

Manning, Harvey. *The Mount Rainier National Park.* Seattle: Superior Publishing Company, n.d.

————. *The North Cascades National Park.* Seattle: Superior Publishing Company, 1969.

Marshall, Louise B. *High Trails, Guide to the Pacific Crest Trail in Washington,* 1973, Signpost, Lynnwood, Washington.

Martin, Jim. *Guidebook to the Feather River Country.* Los Angeles: Ward Ritchie Press, 1972.

Molenaar, Dee. *The Challenge of Rainier.* Seattle: The Mountaineers, 1971.

Muir, John. *The Mountains of California.* Garden City, N.Y.: Doubleday and Company, 1961.

————. *The Yosemite.* Garden City, N.Y.: Doubleday and Company, 1962.

Parker, Horace. *Anza-Borrego Desert Guide Book.* Balboa Island, Calif. Paisano Press, Inc., 1969.

Peterson, P. Victor. *Native Trees of Southern California.* Berkeley and Los Angeles, Calif.: University of California Press, 1970.

Raven, Peter H. *Native Shrubs of Southern California.* Berkeley and Los Angeles, Calif.: University of California Press, 1970.

Robinson, Douglas, Ed. *Starr's Guide to the John Muir Trail and the High Sierra Region.* San Francisco: Sierra Club, 1974.

Rogers, Warren L., Ed. *The PCT Relays.* Santa Ana, Calif.: Camp Research, 1968.

Rolle, Andrew F. *California: A History.* New York: Thomas Y. Crowell Company, 1963.

Schaffer, Jeff, and Hartline, Bev and Fred. *The Pacific Crest Trail, Volume 2: Oregon and Washington.* Berkeley, Calif.: Wilderness Press, 1974.

Schumacher, Genny, Ed. *Deepest Valley, Guide to Owens Valley and its Mountain Lakes, Roadsides, and Trails.* San Francisco: Sierra Club, 1962.

Sharp, Robert P. *Geology Field Guide to Southern California.* Dubuque, Ia.: William C. Brown Company, 1972.

Spring, Ira, and Manning, Harvey. *50 Hikes in Mount Rainier National Park.* Seattle: Mount Rainier Natural History Association and The Mountaineers, 1969.

————. *Wilderness Trails Northwest.* Beaverton, Ore.: The Touchstone Press, 1974.

Storer, Tracy I., and Usinger, Robert L., *Sierra Nevada Natural History.* Berkeley and Los Angeles, Calif.: University of California Press, 1963.

Sunset Books, Ed. *Gold Rush Country.* Menlo Park, Calif.: Lane Books, 1972.

Sutton, Ann and Myron. *Wilderness Areas of North America.* New York: Funk and Wagnalls Company, 1974.

Teale, Edwin Way, Ed. *The Wilderness World of John Muir.* Boston: Houghton Mifflin Company, 1954.

Voge, Harvey H. *A Climber's Guide to the High Sierra.* San Francisco: Sierra Club, 1965.

Webster, Paul. *The Mighty Sierra: Portrait of a Mountain World.* Palo Alto, Calif.: American West Publishing Company, 1972.

Williams, Howel. *Crater Lake, the Story of its Origin.* Berkeley, Calif.: University of California Press, 1972.

Winnett, Thomas. *The Pacific Crest Trail, Volume 1: California.* Berkeley, Calif.: Wilderness Press, 1973.

Wood, Robert S. *Desolation Wilderness.* Berkeley, Calif.: Wilderness Press, 1970.

Yocom, Charles, and Brown, Vinson. *Wildlife and Plants of the Cascades.* Healdsburg, Calif.: Naturegraph Publishers, 1971.

Index

Page numbers in italics refer to illustrations.

227